lonely planet

Diving & Snorkeling

Papua New Guinea

Bob Halstead

Tim Rock

LONELY PLANET PUBLICATIONS
Melbourne • Oakland • London • Paris

Diving & Snorkeling Papua New Guinea
- A Lonely Planet Pisces Book

1st Edition
July, 1999

Published by
Lonely Planet Publications
192 Burwood Road, Hawthorn, Victoria 3122, Australia

Other offices
150 Linden Street, Oakland, California 94607, USA
10A Spring Place, London NW5 3BH, UK
1 rue du Dahomey, 75011 Paris, France

Photographs
by Bob Halstead, Tammy Peluso, Tim Rock, Rocky Roe

Front cover photograph
Eastern Fields, by Bob Halstead

Back cover photographs
Commensal crab on a sea cucumber, by Craig de Wit
Sing-sing man in colorful dress, by Tim Rock
Forward deck of the *S'Jacob*, by Bob Halstead

Many of the images in this guide are available for licensing
from **Lonely Planet Images**
email: lpi@lonelyplanet.com.au

ISBN 0 86442 776 X

text & maps © Lonely Planet 1999
photographs © photographers as indicated 1999

Printed by H&Y Printing Ltd., Hong Kong

Although the authors
and publisher have tried
to make the information
as accurate as possible,
they accept no responsi-
bility for any loss, injury
or inconvenience sus-
tained by any person
using this book.

Contents

Authors

Bob Halstead

Bob has a B.S., Honors degree in physics/mathematics from King's College London University and a post graduate Certificate in Education from Bristol University. He learned to dive in the Bahamas in 1968 and became a NAUI Diving Instructor in 1970. Bob has been exploring PNG's underwater wilderness ever since. Bob and his wife Dinah, PNG's first qualified diving instructor, formed PNG's first full-time sport diving business, Tropical Diving Adventures. In 1986, they started the first live-aboard dive boat operation with the *Telita*.

RUTH PETZOLD

Bob discovered several marine species new to science and has won many international underwater photographic competitions. He has written numerous articles and guides on PNG diving. His latest work includes an educational book published for PNG youth entitled, *The Coral Reefs of Papua New Guinea*. Bob and Dinah live in Australia. They have a fish—*Trichonotus halstead*—named after them.

Bob Halstead's photographic equipment includes Nikonos cameras, Nikon F3 cameras in Aquatica housings and Ikelite 150 strobes.

Tim Rock

Tim attended the journalism program at the University of Nebraska, Omaha. He has spent much of the last 25 years as a professional broadcast and print photojournalist in the Western and Indo Pacific. His television series *Aquaquest Micronesia* was an Ace Award finalist. He has produced six documentaries of the region. Tim is the author of four other Lonely Planet/Pisces diving and snorkeling guides to Palau, Bali and the Komodo Region, Guam & Yap and Chuuk, Pohnpei and Kosrae. Tim lives on Guam with his wife Larie.

LARIE PANGELINAN

Tim Rock's photographic equipment includes Nikonos II, III, IV & V cameras, housed Nikons in Aquatica housings and Nikonos RSAF cameras and lenses. His strobes are made by Nikon and Ikelite.

From the Authors

The authors wish to thank the following divers and friends who helped compile information for this book:

Dr. Chris Acott, Dietmar Amon, Kevin Baldwin, Mike Ball, Franco Banfi, David Barker, Peter Barter, Telita Bates, Max Benjamin, Michael Burden, Frank Butler, Chris Carney, Owen Coney, Craig de Wit, James Elijah, Barry Fitzpatrick, Dave Flinn, Peter Jennings, Tony Karasconyi, Linda Kavanagh, Mary Jane Kelly, Dik Knight, Peter Leggett, John Lippmann, Peter Manz, David Miller, Geoff Murphy, Susy O'Connell, Rob Padfield, Tammy Peluso, Rodney Pearce, Alan Rabbe, Tim Rowlands, Nikhil Sekhran, Peter Stone, Ken Weaving. They'd also like to thank Neil Whiting for the use of his Bootless Bay wreck illustrations that appear in his book *Wrecks and Reefs*, which is about Port Moresby diving.

Bob Halstead would especially like to thank his wife Dinah. "She has shared the adventure of exploring PNG's underwater paradise with me, shown me exquisite creatures I would otherwise have missed and blessed me with her love and laughter."

Tim Rock would also like to thank his wife Larie, "...whose encouragement and support, despite living in a house overflowing with slides, has allowed me to wander the Pacific, experiencing a truly a fantastic world."

From the Publisher

This first edition was published in Lonely Planet's U.S. office under the guidance of Roslyn Bullas, the "Divemaster" of Pisces Books. From the coral-encrusted Fish Tank, "Dogfish" Debra Miller edited the text and photos, while "Super Grouper" Emily Douglas designed the book and cover. Navigating nautical charts was cartographer Patrick Bock, who created the maps. Hayden Foell plunged in to illustrate the underwater wrecks. Carto Capt. Alex Guilbert and "Sharky" Scott Summers provided help along the way.

Bill Alevizon reviewed the marine life sections for scientific accuracy. Portions of the text were adapted from Lonely Planet's *Papua New Guinea* and from Asian Diver's *ScubaGuide Papua New Guinea*. Thanks also to Tim Rock and Bob Halstead for their good humor, quick responses and for rarely rubbing in the fact they live in the tropics.

Lonely Planet Pisces Books

Lonely Planet acquired the Pisces line of diving and snorkeling books in 1997. The series is being developed and substantially revamped over the next few years. We invite your comments and suggestions.

Pisces Pre-Dive Safety Guidelines

Before embarking on a scuba diving, skin diving or snorkeling trip, ensure a safe and enjoyable experience by giving careful consideration to the following:

- Possess a current diving certification card from a recognized scuba diving instructional agency (if scuba diving)
- Be sure you are healthy and feel comfortable diving
- Obtain reliable information about physical and environmental conditions at the dive site (e.g. from a reputable local dive operation)
- Be aware of local laws, regulations, and etiquette about marine life and environment
- Dive at sites within your experience level; if available, engage the services of a competent, professionally trained dive instructor or dive master

Underwater conditions vary significantly from one region, or even site, to another. Seasonal changes can significantly alter any site and dive conditions. These differences influence the way divers dress for a dive and what diving techniques they use.

Regardless of location, there are special requirements for diving in that area. Before your dive, ask about the environmental characteristics that can affect your diving and how local, trained divers deal with these considerations.

Warning & Request

Even with dive guides, things change—dive site conditions, regulations, topside information. Nothing stays the same for long. Your feedback on this book will be used to help update future editions and make the next edition more useful. Excerpts from your correspondence may appear in our newsletter, Planet Talk, or in the Postcards section of our website. Please let us know if your don't want your letter published or your name acknowledged.

Correspondence can be addressed to:
Lonely Planet Publications
Pisces Books
150 Linden Street
Oakland, CA 94607
e-mail: pisces@lonelyplanet.com

Introduction

TIM ROCK

To many, it is the last frontier on Earth. When all else seems explored, exploited and overpopulated, Papua New Guinea (known herein as PNG) continues to hold mystery, excitement and adventure. Indeed, it has been aptly deemed "The Land of Adventure." PNG has no trouble at all living up to its reputation as one of the most exciting countries in the world to explore.

If you fly in from the south, over the deep purple of the Coral Sea and Great Barrier Reef, you'll notice that the young mountains ridging the mainland are sharp and sheer. They were created from coral limestone when the Australian continent broke from Antarctica, slid north, and collided with the island of New Guinea. If you fly in from the north, you'll see the terrain rising to the clouds and then plunging deep into the lush jungles, again and again. Great fertile valleys carry tropical rain—even melted snow—to the coast, sometimes via rivers that may be navigated for hundreds of kilometers, elsewhere through huge areas of savanna or swamp.

Time has not rounded the edges of the rugged mountain ranges. Hundreds of volcanoes—many still active—sculpt the landscape with gentler curves and cones.

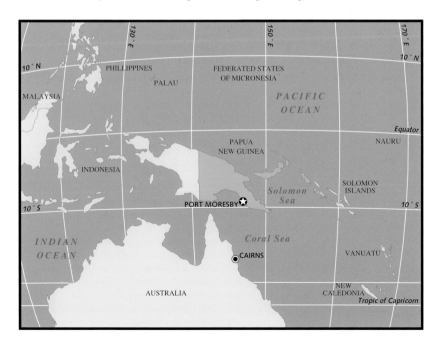

Wild rapids plunging through chasmic gorges become calm drifting waters whose quiet is drowned out by the clamor of birds and insects in the surrounding jungles.

This remarkable geography tends to isolate tribes of people. Many weren't exposed to the outside world until just a few decades ago. Striking photographs published in international magazines portrayed PNG's tribal people clad in feathered costume with painted faces and bodies; they became a famous and inspiring intrigue throughout the world.

The character of the people match the bounty of the land. Rich in culture and language, Papua New Guineans are colorful and diverse. The greater part of the population still live traditional lifestyles in the villages. The days of marauding headhunters and isolated territorialism are all but gone, but the tribal gatherings and simple dwellings visitors can still meet the "Real PNG."

Do not judge the country by its larger towns. For the most part, they are a mess—desperate monuments of the rush into the modern world. Sadly, traditional beliefs were discarded before the means to survive in an alien, urban environment were learned. Confusion reigns. Back in the villages, however, people possess a natural generosity and hospitality that would put most western countries to shame.

This Garden of Eden certainly has its snakes, but also some remarkable flora and fauna. PNG is home to 38 of the world's 43 spectacular species of birds of paradise (the bird appears on the national flag), wallabies, cuscus, bats and has a biodiversity to match the variety of its landscapes.

The coasts and coral islands offer a different vision of South Pacific splendor. No birds of paradise in these lowlands, but perhaps Paradise itself—palm-fringed shores are decorated with orchids, butterflies, colorful parrots and cockatoos.

Dive sites listed in this book are broken down into nine regions: Port Moresby, Milne Bay, D'Entrecasteaux Islands & Tufi, Lae, Madang, Kimbe Bay, Rabaul, Kavieng and Remote Islands. In addition to descriptions of the type of diving and marine life you can expect, you'll get specific weather information for each area and an overview of the distinct geographic and cultural attributes unique to each region.

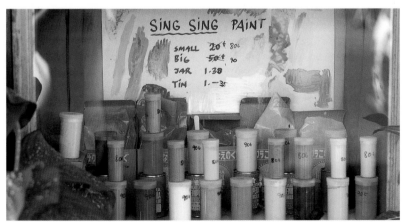

Celebratory *sing-sing* paint for sale at a Boroko market.

Overview

ROCKY ROE

Loloata Island

PNG consists of the eastern half of the island of New Guinea and the islands of New Britain, Bougainville and the Bismark Archipelago. The most northerly point is the uninhabited Sae Island and the most southerly Tagula Island in the Louisiade Archipelago. Westernmost PNG borders with Irian Jaya, a province of Indonesia. To the south is Australia and to the east, the Solomon Islands. PNG is spread over 1,200km (746 miles) from north to south and over 2,000km (1,243 miles) west to east. It is estimated that there are over 600 islands in PNG.

The population is about 4.5 million, 35% of whom live in the Central Highlands region. A large mountain range runs like a spine through the middle of the mainland with several peaks rising to over 4,000m (13,000ft). The interior terrain is extremely rugged and sparsely populated outside the Highland's valleys.

The people are predominantly Melanesian with some Polynesian, Micronesian, Asian and European influences. Although most of the people still live by traditional subsistence farming and barter, PNG also has a vibrant, modern economy based mainly on its rich mineral deposits. The main exports are gold, copper, oil, coffee, tea, copra, palm oil, timber and marine products.

Christianity is the official PNG religion (forged in the Nation's Constitution) and missionaries have largely stamped out traditional spiritual beliefs of the people, although some beliefs survive. There is freedom of religious expression in PNG.

TIM ROCK

Copra plantations stretch down to the shoreline on Bagabag Island.

11

History

Settlement of New Guinea and Irian Jaya dates back 50,000 years, when the island was actually a land-bridge still connected to Australia. The bridge allowed people to migrate from Southeast Asia through Australia and into parts of PNG. Carbon dating reveals that these first settlers were quite innovative: stone axes date back as far as 40,000 years. Evidence of Highlands habitation goes back 30,000 years and shows Highlanders gardening 9,000 years ago, making them among the first farmers on the planet. Oddly, one of PNG's most populous areas today, the south coast, was last to be settled.

All historical records were, for the most part, oral. There is little documentation of the country's history. Migrations were mostly traced through language. For example, Austronesian languages, similar to those in other parts of the Pacific, are spoken by people who settled on the coast and, through trade, maintained contact with the outside world.

Eventually tribes and clans became separate and distinct, living in their own micro-worlds and developing unique cultural differences. This is what European explorers found they first stumbled upon PNG.

When the world's climate warmed 6,000 years ago, seas rose. This isolated the huge island. From the 1600s to the 1900s, the Dutch, Germans, English and finally the Australians, laid claim to various parts of the country. Australia and Great Britain eventually won out after WWI.

TIM ROCK

WWII wrecks rest above and below the sea, including this Japanese bomber in Madang.

In 1926, gold was discovered. Four years later prospectors stumbled upon tribal Highlanders. These people, numbering over a million at the time, had had no prior contact with Europeans or Australians.

WWII brought the Japanese to PNG and, by 1942, they occupied and established bases throughout the country. The Japanese effort didn't last long, but it still took three years and many bloody battles for the Australians to reclaim the main island.

Following the war, many Australians moved to PNG. Today, the ex-pat population is estimated at 24,000.

Australia followed world opinion denouncing colonialism, and PNG gained full independence in 1975. Today economic concerns conflicting with environmental and social needs confront the government, which is struggling to provide and maintain infrastructure, education and financial growth for PNG's burgeoning population.

An Island farmer comes out to the boat to sell bananas and coconuts.

Geography

Mainland PNG's geographic profile, with a mountainous backbone descending into coastal waters, is replicated on a smaller scale on the eastern islands.

The eroding power of the country's two major rivers, the Sepik and the Strickland, has combined with frequent earthquakes to create a massive gash in the grassland corridor, known as the Strickland Gorge. The Sepik basin was once an extensive inland sea. During floods, the Sepik's water spills onto a massive flood plain. To the south, the Fly River is almost as impressive and flows into the Gulf of Papua.

The large rivers spew a constant flood of muddy water into the ocean so not until just before Port Moresby is the coastal water clear enough for coral reefs to survive. The larger islands to the east have similar topography, although some east of New Ireland are the peaks of a submerged volcanic mountain chain. The Trobriand and Muyua (Woodlark) islands are raised coral atolls.

Diving History

The first divers in PNG were hard-hat pearl divers who worked the lucrative pearling grounds in Milne Bay before WWII. After the war, the many sunken wrecks attracted adventurers who salvaged the valuable brass and bronze.

Sport diving started up in the 1960s. In 1977 PNG's first full-time dive school opened in Port Moresby. The first live-aboard, *Telita*, started operating in 1986.

Many areas in the country are unexplored or have been dived by just a handful of local divers. The total number of divers visiting every year is so few that most of the popular dive sites do not see more than 200 divers a year. This contrasts dramatically with reefs in other parts of the world where degradation is obvious and inevitable, no matter how many rules of dive etiquette are enforced.

PNG reefs are mainly damaged not by divers but by weather, outbreaks of coral-eating sea stars or mollusks, or even reef-eating fish. The reefs can repair themselves from this natural damage rapidly. PNG is fortunate to be one of the few places left in the world where nature is the predominant force affecting her reefs.

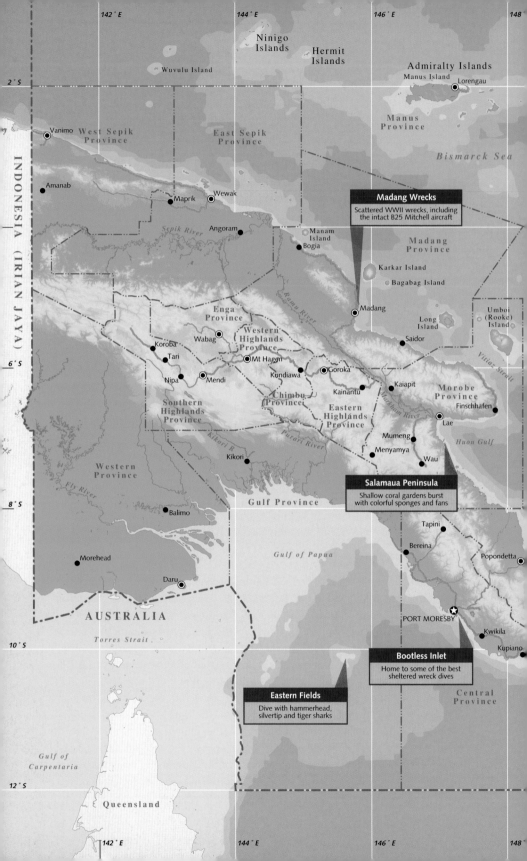

Ninigo
Islands

Hermit
Islands

Admiralty Islands
Manus Island   Lorengau

2°S

Wuvulu Island

Vanimo   West Sepik
Province

East Sepik
Province

Manus
Province

Bismarck Sea

INDONESIA (IRIAN JAYA)

Amanab

Maprik   Wewak

Angoram

Sepik River

Manam
Island
Bogia

Madang Wrecks

Scattered WWII wrecks, including
the intact B25 Mitchell aircraft

Madang
Province

Karkar Island

Bagabag Island

Madang

Long
Island

Saidor

Umboi
(Rooke)
Island

Enga
Province

Koroba
Tari

Wabag

Western
Highlands
Province

Ramu River

6°S

Nipa   Mendi

Mt Hagen

Kundiawa

Goroka

Kainantu

Kaiapit

Morobe
Province

Finschhafen

Vitiaz Strait

Southern
Highlands
Province

Chimbu
Province

Eastern
Highlands
Province

Markham River

Lae

Huon Gulf

Western
Province

Kikori R.

Purari River

Kikori

Mumeng
Menyamya

Wau

Salamaua Peninsula

Shallow coral gardens burst
with colorful sponges and fans

8°S

Fly River

Balimo

Gulf Province

Gulf of Papua

Tapini

Bereina

Popondetta

Morehead

Daru

AUSTRALIA

PORT MORESBY

Kwikila

Kupiano

10°S

Torres Strait

Bootless Inlet

Home to some of the best
sheltered wreck dives

Central
Province

Eastern Fields

Dive with hammerhead,
silvertip and tiger sharks

Gulf of
Carpentaria

12°S

Queensland

142°E   144°E   146°E   148°

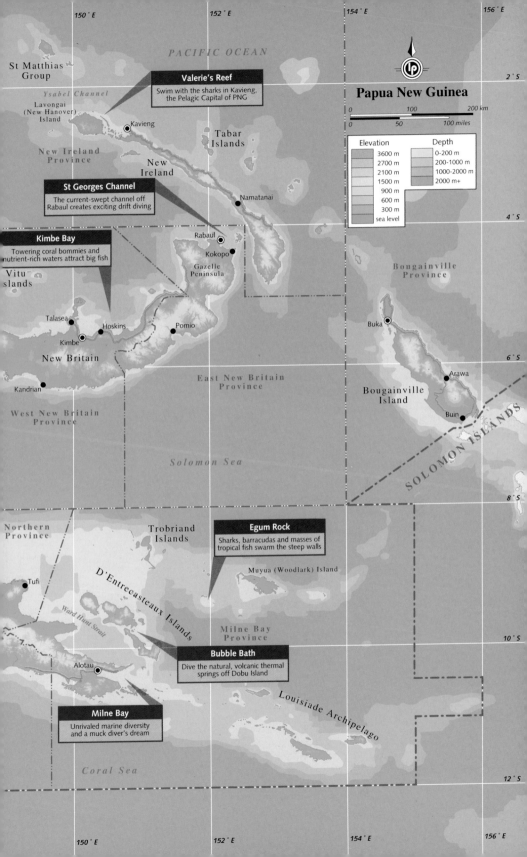

PACIFIC OCEAN

St Matthias
Group

Ysabel Channel

Lavongai
(New Hanover)
Island

● Kavieng

Tabar
Islands

New Ireland
Province

New
Ireland

Namatanai ●

Valerie's Reef
Swim with the sharks in Kavieng,
the Pelagic Capital of PNG

St Georges Channel
The current-swept channel off
Rabaul creates exciting drift diving

Kimbe Bay
Towering coral bommies and
nutrient-rich waters attract big fish

Vitu
Islands

Talasea ●
● Hoskins
Kimbe ●
New Britain

Kandrian ●

West New Britain
Province

Rabaul ●
● Kokopo
Gazelle
Peninsula

Pomio ●

East New Britain
Province

Solomon Sea

Bougainville Island

Buka ●

Bougainville
Province

Arawa ●

Bougainville
Island

Buin ●

SOLOMON ISLANDS

Papua New Guinea

Elevation	Depth
3600 m	0-200 m
2700 m	200-1000 m
2100 m	1000-2000 m
1500 m	2000 m+
900 m	
600 m	
300 m	
sea level	

0   100   200 km
0   50   100 miles

Northern
Province

Tufi ●

Trobriand
Islands

D'Entrecasteaux Islands

Egum Rock
Sharks, barracudas and masses of
tropical fish swarm the steep walls

Muyua (Woodlark) Island

Ward Hunt Strait

Milne Bay
Province

Bubble Bath
Dive the natural, volcanic thermal
springs off Dobu Island

Alotau ●

Milne Bay
Unrivaled marine diversity
and a muck diver's dream

Louisiade Archipelago

Coral Sea

150° E   152° E   154° E   156° E

2° S

4° S

6° S

8° S

10° S

12° S

TIM ROCK

Practicalities

Climate

The coastal climate is tropical but quite variable around the coast. It is generally hot, humid and wet year round. Rainfall is heavy but varies greatly. In some areas heavy rains last a few months, followed by a distinct dry spell. Other areas receive a fairly even spread. In extreme rainfall areas, annual rainfall can average more than 8m (315 inches)! The wet season is roughly from December to March, the dry season from May to October. PNG rarely suffers the direct force of cyclones, although developing cyclones sometimes pass through the eastern Louisiade Archipelago. Cyclones in the Coral Sea may affect the weather on the south coast.

Average surface sea temperatures vary between 25°C (77°F) along the edge of the Coral Sea to the 29°C (84°F) common in the Bismarck Sea. Topside coastal temperatures hover around 25°C to 30°C (77°F to 86°F).

Language

More than 770 languages are spoken in PNG—about one-third of the world's indigenous languages. English is the official language for business, education and government, but *Tok Pisin*—or Pidgin—is the second language of most Papua New Guineans.

TIM ROCK

Pidgin Chatter

Learning some rudimentary Pidgin is not as tough as you might think and will earn you considerable bonus points with the locals. Written Pidgin is very phonetic and many words sound like their English counterparts. The following words and phrases provide some of the basics for communication in *Tok Pisin*:

Good Morning	Moning tru	Yes . . . Yes	No . . . Nogat
Good Afternoon	Apinun tru	scuba dive	swim aninit long sol wara
Thank you	Tenkyu	strong current	taid I stong tumas
Please	Plis	high tide	si kam antap
How are you	Yu stap gut?	low tide	si I go daun
I'm fine	Mi stap gut	clear water	klin wara
What is your name?	Wanem nem bilong yu?	dirty water	doti wara
See you later	Lukim yu behain	coral	rip
I do not understand	mi no save	boat	bot
Do you understand?	yu save?	ship	sip

Getting There

Although there are some wild and wonderful ways of getting to PNG, almost everybody comes by air. The vast majority of flights come to Port Moresby from Australia, although you can get direct connections from Singapore, Manila (the Philippines), Hong Kong, Honiara (Solomon Islands), Jayapura (Irian Jaya) and connecting flights from Tokyo (Japan).

Air Niugini, the national airline, operates in conjunction with a number of other airlines. Port Moresby is by far the largest international gateway to PNG, but there are also international flights to Mt. Hagen. Air Niugini: P.O. Box 7186, Boroko, PNG ☎ 675 325 9000 Fax: 675 327 3482, www.airniugini.com.pg

Getting Around

Geographic realities continue to rule on PNG: the scattered population, often isolated in mountain valleys and on tiny islands, renders public transportion limited to local and regional destinations. PNG has no train services, expressways, highways or main roads that connect the entire country, so the predominent method of travel between the main centers is by air. Many smaller airlines operate throughout the country with scheduled flights and charter services. The largest of these is: **Milne Bay Air**, P.O. Box 170 Boroko, PNG ☎ 675 325 0555 Fax: 675 325 2219.

Locally, taxis are available and there are many converted trucks and buses licensed as Public Motor Vehicles. The acronym PMV is widely used, mostly preceded by an expletive, particularly by other motorists.

Entry Requirements & Customs

Visas: A 60-day tourist visa is available on arrival for a fee of K25. This cannot be extended. Restrictions apply for travelers from some Asian, Eastern European and African countries. For longer stays, or peace of mind, a visa may be obtained before you depart for PNG. All tourists must have sufficient funds, a valid passport and a return ticket. A tax of K30 is payable upon departure. This must be paid in kinos. **Customs:** Importation of guns, ammunition, pornography and narcotic drugs is strictly prohibited. Diving tourists can bring their own diving and photographic equipment into PNG on the understanding that it will be taken out upon departure. It may be useful to have a list of the equipment with you, particularly if several cameras are involved.

Money

The unit of currency is the kina (pronounced Key-nuh), which is divided into 100 toea (pronounced Toy-ah). The value of the kina fluctuates wildly, which will likely continue for some time to come.

American Express and MasterCard are widely accepted in the towns, but many of the smaller diving operators do not accept credit cards at all. Banking in PNG can be a slow affair, but it is possible to transfer money, cash traveler's checks and exchange money.

Time

PNG time is 10 hours ahead of GMT. When it's noon in PNG, it is the same time in Sydney, 2am in London and 6pm the day before in San Francisco. There is no adjustment for Daylight Saving Time in PNG.

Electricity

240 volts, 50 Hz. with Australian-style sockets of two or three flat pins angled to each other. Many resorts and boats have 120 Volts (50 Hz) with U.S.-style sockets available. Adapters are available in Port Moresby is some electronics stores.

Weights & Measures

The metric system is standard. In this book, both imperial and metric measurements are given, except for specific references to depth, which are given in meters.

What to Bring

Topside: Wear lightweight clothing that will protect you from the sun and insects. Women should not wear short shorts or bikini bottoms in public as they will invite ridicule and may offend locals. A windbreaker or shell is helpful in the rainy season or when the trade winds are blowing.

Underwater: Divers usually bring their own equipment except tanks and weights, but gear is available for rental at most land-based resorts, although not on liveaboards. Most ships carry some spare gear for emergencies. Rental equipment is usually a major brand name and in good repair. Divers use thin wetsuits or dive skins mostly for protection from sunburn, coral cuts or abrasions. Thicker wetsuits are sometimes required in the south during winter months.

Underwater Photography & Video

Photographers should bring their own color slide film, video tapes, batteries and equipment. Limited supplies are available only in Port Moresby at **Images** ☎ 325 5106, Fax: 325 3835 and at **PNG Colour Lab** ☎ 325 4665, Fax: 325 0358, which also provides E6 processing.

Walindi Diving and the *Paradise Sport* now have resident photo pros and a nice range of rental equipment. Instruction, specialty courses, E6 processing or videos of your dive or trip can be arranged. Loloata Island Resort can arrange for daily E6 or print film processing. There is no camera repair facility in PNG. Camera sales are limited, so bring back-up bodies and lenses.

Business Hours

Business hours are normally 8am to 5pm, Monday through Friday. Shopping marts and some stores in larger towns may stay open a little later in the evenings. Markets open around 9am and vary on closing times. Banks are open from 9am to 4:30pm weekdays and until 5pm on Fridays.

Accommodations

The largest and greatest variety of accommodations are found in the Port Moresby area. The quantity and range of hotels decreases markedly outside of the capital city. Traditionally, hotel rates in PNG are not cheap, although it varies, depending on the strength or weakness of the fluctuating Kina. Most major hotels accept Visa, MasterCard and American Express.

Many resorts cater to divers and have a dive shop, boat or boats and an instructor or divemaster on staff. The many live-aboards cater specifically to divers and can arrange or recommend land-based accommodations and activities.

A few native-style, extremely basic homestays and accommodations are available. Divers with equipment should make arrangements to store their equipment somewhere as these are normally quite interesting and rustic overnights but not truly secure or set up for diving.

Dining & Food

Excellent restaurants serve an international cuisine in most of the main centers. Basic supplies can be purchased at local trade stores and excellent fruit and vegetables are available from the many local markets. Bottled water is sold in towns, however tap water is usually good to drink. Take any opportunity to join a village feast, which might feature a *mumu*, or traditional underground oven, where herb-wrapped vegetables and beef are cooked on hot stones. Alcoholic beverages, except for the splendid PNG beer, are very expensive.

Shopping

Due to the lack of contact between different villages and groups of people, PNG arts are a rich and potent representation of national heritage and indigenous tradition. Artifacts are highly prized and can be purchased locally at markets, stores, your hotel, or at specialty stores in Port Moresby. Shopping in PNG can be pricey so look out for stores such as **PNG Arts** in Port Moresby, which is largely regarded to have competitive pricing. Madang's market and a small market near the Madang Resort also have some nice handicrafts from the Sepik region and occasionally from the highlands. Carvings, woven bags or *bilums* (string bags), shell necklaces, books and videos on PNG, jewelry and other items are available. Do not buy products created from endangered species—such as anything made with turtle shell or black coral.

Bargaining is common in some parts of PNG and considered insulting in others. Check with a local guide to see whether bargaining is common or expected in the area you're visiting.

TIM ROCK

A bilum bag full of coconuts.

TIM ROCK

Activities & Attractions

While diving is one of the main tourist activities in PNG, most visitors come to experience the dramatic untouched landscapes and unique cultures of its people.

A number of nature preserves—called Wildlife Management Areas—are starting to pop up as the need to conserve and preserve the local wildlife becomes more apparent. The National Wildlife Division can tell you if you're going to a preservation area.

The concept of national parks is a fairly new one in PNG, but there are now three, including the **Varirata National Park** near Port Moresby, **McAdam National Park** near Lae, and **Lake Kutubu** in the Southern Highlands.

Guided tours are available in many parts of the country, particularly along the Sepik River and in the Highland areas. Visiting divers may have to make special arrangements to travel to the Highlands as they are off the beaten flight path to most coastal harbors. A Sepik River adventure is well worth it, but requires some planning ahead.

If you're not into hauling gear all over the country, take in one of the annual cultural shows in the main centers. Different clans come together to celebrate and display their cultural heritage in good-natured competition. These are still authentic shows and can be incredibly rewarding to watch.

Other adventurous watersport activities include windsurfing, sailing and canoeing. Game fishing is a growing activity and includes freshwater fishing for bass and barramundi, as well as classic big game fishing for billfish and tuna. Surfing beaches are available around Wewak and Kavieng.

Port Moresby

The **Hiri Moale Festival** (starts September 16th) is held in conjunction with other Independence Day celebrations. At this traditional celebration—or *sing-sing*—dance groups gather wearing the traditional garb and paint that PNG is famous for. Another *sing-sing* is held in June to celebrate the Queen of England's birthday.

Varirata National Park is outside of town up the Laloki River Valley. It is PNG's first national park and has varied and well-marked trails. Varirata bisects the arduous Kokoda Trail, which takes several days, involves staying in villages and provides real insight to PNG art and life. The trail re-traces the route between Port Moresby and the north coast along which a bloody battle was fought in WWII.

Varirata is also famous for its birdwatching. June to November is reportedly bird of paradise season. Also visit Rouna Falls overlook, which is on the way to the park. Bluffs provide lookouts to sunsets, the city and the sea coastline.

The **National Botanic Gardens** are a real showcase for the city. Moresby is located on the dry side of the landmass and it is normally brown about half the year; however, north of the university at the gardens, the tropics come alive. This serendipitous place has more than 2km of boardwalks that wander under the jungle canopies. Finely manicured lawns and displays of both rare and exotic flora scent the jungle. Orchid lovers will want to see the native and hybrid plants that have been raised here.

Bomana War Cemetery is where history buffs come to appreciate the sacrifices of war. Over 4,000 Australian and Papua New Guinean soldiers and war casualties are buried here.

For politicos, a visit to the **National Parliament Building** can be entertaining, especially when lawmakers are in session and are heatedly debating an issue. The building itself is beautiful—made of local wood— and rises high with a traditional pitched roof.

Ela Beach lines the main drag and is easily accessed. It offers sailing, canoe races and paddling races in huge outriggers. Kids like to play in the normally placid waves.

TIM ROCK

Children at Ela Beach.

Milne Bay

Samarai Island was once the administrative center for Milne Bay province and the largest town in PNG. Known as the Pearl of the Pacific, the island was the meeting place for missionaries, adventurers and administration. It has a colorful history, though today it is quiet and somewhat derelict.

The people are still as friendly as ever and every year stage the **Pearl Festival** (or Milne Bay Show) on the Independence Day holiday. Villagers gather from the surrounding islands to celebrate their culture.

Kwato Island was the home of famous missionary Charles Abel, and the mission he established still thrives. Visitors are welcome and can walk to the top of the hill where a lovingly constructed church looks out over the islands of China Strait.

Alotau took over where Samarai Island left off and is now the main government and commercial center for the province. The town market adjoins the **Alice Wedega Park** and there is a nice overlook of the village at the hospital. Alotau isn't really set up for tourists, so organized activities aren't readily available.

Another attraction are the ancient **Skull Caves**, where the skulls of raiding warriors were stored after their defeat. Villagers can show you the storage places for these human skulls. Lives are more peaceful these days and tribal fighting does not take place here as it still does in the Highlands.

BOB HALSTEAD

Skulls of tribal warriors are stored in caves.

D'Entrecasteaux & Tufi

The hot springs at Kedidia on **Fergusson Island** are well worth a visit. A guide from the nearby village will take you to an area of bubbling mud pools, steaming streams. A lively geyser will shoot high into the sky, apparently on command of the village. Mineral-caked paths hide boiling pools. Take care to heed the directions of your guide.

Dobu Island, its cone shape obviously a dormant volcano, was an early Methodist mission station. It has an interesting old church and very friendly villagers who welcome visitors. The thermal springs on Dobu are also worth a visit.

Tufi has a "**King Fish Season**" where Spanish mackerel are abundant. The fishing is considered excellent and can be arranged with the Tufi Resort. Walks along the fjord ridges are worthwhile for their stunning views. Tapa cloth made from bark is sold at modest prices.

Lae

Although Lae's **botanical gardens**—once the finest in the country—have been superseded by Port Moresby's superb new gardens, they are still worth a visit. You can visit the **War Cemetery** at the same time, where the numbers of graves are a devastating reminder of the tragedy of war.

Lae has a tiny and crowded harbor but the **yacht club** welcomes visitors and can provide information on getting over to Salamaua Island.

McAdam National Park is between the towns of Wau and Bulolo. Rich, stream-fed, lowland rain forest stretches up to 1000m and then becomes varied hardwood forest with lots of accompanying wildlife. There is only one trail through this park. Foot travel is the best way to glimpse echidnas, cuscuses, the large cassowaries, birds of paradise, eagles and even the increasingly rare tree kangaroo. Orchids, ferns and butterflies thrive here as well.

TIM ROCK

The hornbill is one of the more unusual birds found in PNG.

In Wau and Bulolo, remnants of the huge gold mine dredges can still be seen. The **Wau Ecology Institute** boasts a butterfly farm, where some of the world's most lovely butterflies are bred. Other insects are available (dead and framed) for sale.

If that doesn't tickle your weird side, you could go to **Aseki**, where a collection of mummified bodies of PNG ancestors can be viewed and photographed for a fee.

Lae is the starting point for the Highlands Highway. Adventurers can drive the highway into the heart of the PNG Highlands.

Madang

A visit to a unique village where **Yabob pottery** is handmade and fired in village ovens is a must. This pottery is known throughout the region and people travel for many kilometers to trade goods and foods for the prized red clay vessels.

For a great side trip after a week of live-aboard cruising, find out about taking a **Sepik River Cruise**. This can be an incredible journey up one of the world largest and most fascinating rivers. The Sepik is to PNG what the Congo is to Africa or the Amazon to South America. Witnessing the unique river lifestyles, the people and their many tribal crafts, is truly worth the extra time and expense.

In town, the **Cultural Center/Madang Visitors Bureau** has some very nice Highland displays that show Sepik canoes, war and dance masks, shields and instruments. There is a breathtaking overlook of the peninsula from the **Lutheran grounds**.

TIM ROCK

Madang sulphur springs.

Kimbe Bay

The **crocodile farm** near the airport has some smaller reptiles but also some very large creatures that bring Jurassic thoughts when they come into view. Timber and especially palm oil are the big exports here, but the crocodile farm is a newer sidelight and a good way to preserve the saltwater crocodile in the tropics. These reptiles actually perform an important function, aerating mangrove areas and keeping on top of the food chain.

Talasea Hot Springs is a worthwhile trip. After a week or so of constant diving, a good soaking in these bubbling waters makes all the aches and pains recede. Local people swear by it, and they have to work the copra and oil plantations.

Talasea is also a center for **shell money**. This currency plays an important traditional part in the lives of local people. A prospective groom must have a certain amount of shell money to present to his future in-laws before he can obtain a bride. The manufacture of this money is hard, exacting work. Ask if there is any shell money being made while you are in the area. Also, look for any examples of obsidian knives and spearheads that were fashioned in the past.

Rabaul

Rabaul has had a fantastic history, disturbed by two major volcanic eruptions in 1937 and 1994. The main attraction today is the amazing effect of the most recent eruption—much of the township was simply flattened and buried. A series of regular mini eruptions still continues.

Tunnels and **war artifacts** may still be seen in various locations. Guided tours can be arranged to historic sites from the time of Queen Emma who "ruled" before the turn of the century.

The **Japanese War Memorial** is considered the main Japanese memorial for this part of the world. Getting there can be a little precarious as the road is ashed out, but think of it as an adventure.

The Bainings people have a ceremonial **fire dance**. It is one of the most spectacular cultural events in the whole of PNG and should not be missed.

Kavieng

With all of the pelagic action—dogtooth tuna, marlin and tuna—**game fishing** is understandably good in Kavieng. Please remember that catch-and-release is the favored method of fishing in the Pacific.

Lined with history, Kavieng may have had inhabitants as far back as 30,000 years ago and has a datable history going back 12,000 years. The world war years left remnants all over, as the Japanese used New Ireland as a major staging area.

The **Boluminski Highway** is an adventure in itself. Baron Boluminski was the German administrator before the WWI and is famous for building this road along the length of New Ireland. His gravesite can be visited in Kavieng's old cemetery. Remains of the stairway to his grand residence can still be seen near a large Japanese gun on a ridge overlooking the harbor.

Kavieng is famous for its beautiful white sand beaches, some of which produce good **surfing** for experienced surfers.

Remote Islands

The islands refered to in the dive sections are not truly set up for tourism of any sort, and most of the boat trips you'll take here will be specifically for diving. Some islands have inland lakes, some have war artifacts, while others have simply great natural attractions. You can barter for bushwalks to these sites, but don't count on it as an impromptu activity, as the special equipment necessary to travel about here (such as machetes, tents, and heavy doses of mosquito repellent) may not be available.

An old Island fisherman carves a speargun out of coconut wood.

Diving Health & Safety

BOB HALSTEAD

Malaria

Malaria is one of the most serious health concerns in PNG. The mosquito-borne disease can be fatal, so do not take bite protection lightly. Obviously, try to avoid being bitten by mosquitos, which are active at night. Wear protective clothing and apply insect repellent containing DEET. Clothing and nets can be sprayed with a pyrmethrin repellent that lasts for several weeks. Use mosquito nets in places with no electricity. The readily available mortein "Mozzie Zapper," a device that plugs in to the electric socket of your room at night, is highly recommended.

Preventative malaria medication may also be advisable. However, it is not always effective, and divers may have adverse reactions. Mefloquine (Lariam) is specifically not recommended for divers as it may produce side effects that mimic decompression illness. Chloroquine, once the drug of choice, is now less effective because many malaria parasites have developed a resistance to it. Other anti-malarial drugs include doxycycline (which has photosensitizing effects) and a combination of chloroquine and proguanil. One herbal treatment making headway against malaria is artemether, a Chinese medicine the locals swear by. It is not readily available in the U.S. or most European countries, but can be purchased in PNG.

While divers may feel most comfortable taking a pill, most veteran ex-pats will tell you that the side effects from anti-malarial drugs are just not worth it. In fact, many dive operators in PNG will not allow anyone who has taken mefloquine to dive.

Before your trip, consult a physician or a travel medicine clinic. Make sure this business or doctor is familiar with PNG and diving.

Pre-trip Preparation

At least a month before your trip, inspect your dive gear. Your regulator should be serviced annually. Change your dive computer battery before the trip, or get the manufacturer to do it for you.

If possible, find out if your dive operator rents or can service your gear. If not, you might want to take spare parts or spare gear. Purchase any additional equipment you might need, such as a dive light and tank marker light for night diving, a line reel for wreck diving, etc. Make sure you have at least a whistle attached to your BC and, even better, add a marker tube (also known as a safety sausage).

Diving and Flying

Divers to PNG get there by plane. While it's fine to dive soon *after* flying, it's important to remember that your last dive should be completed at least 12 hours (some experts advise 24 hours) *before* your flight to minimize the risk of residual nitrogen in the blood that can cause decompression injury.

About a week before taking off, do a final check of your gear, grease o-rings, check batteries and assemble a save-a-dive kit (and possibly a first aid kit). Don't forget to pack medical prescriptions or medications such as decongestants, ointments for scratches, ear drops, antihistimines and seasickness tablets.

DAN

Divers Alert Network (DAN) is an international membership association of individuals and organizations sharing a common interest in diving and safety. It operates a 24-hour diving emergency hotline in the U.S. at ☎ **919-684-8111** or **919-684-4DAN** (919-684-4DAN (-4326) accepts collect calls in a dive emergency). DAN does not directly provide medical care; however, it does provide advice on early treatment, evacuation, and hyperbaric treatment of diving-related injuries. Divers should contact DAN for assistance as soon as a diving emergency is suspected. DAN membership is reasonably priced and includes DAN TravelAssist, a membership benefit, which covers medical air evacuation from anywhere in the world for any illness or injury. For a small additional fee, divers can get secondary insurance coverage for decompression illness. For membership questions ☎ 800-446-2671 in the U.S. or ☎ 919-684-2948 elsewhere.

Recompression Facilities

There is now a recompression chamber facility in Port Moresby, although you need to be referred before you can get treated. For instance, if a bend situation occurred as a result of a heart attack, the patient would likely not be treated in PNG as hospital facilities are not equipped for this kind of care.

In a diving emergency, contact the Diving Emergency Service (DES) in Australia ☎ 05 61 8 82225771. The DES on-duty doctor will assess the situation and advise a course of action. DAN members needing evacuation should contact DAN TravelAssist ☎ 05-1-202-296-9620, which will arrange all evacuations paid for by DAN. Milne Bay Air provides PNG with Medevac services ☎ 325 2011. Evacuation to the chamber and treatment at the chamber may cost thousands of dollars. All divers should have evacuation *and* treatment insurance before diving.

For after-chamber intensive care, patients will likely be referred to the nearest international facility, **Townsville General Hospital** in Queensland, Australia ☎ 61 0 77819455 Fax: 61 0 77726711.

Deep Diving

Opportunities to dive deep abound in PNG. Many attractions are beyond 40m (130ft), which is considered the maximum depth limit of sport diving. Before venturing beyond these limits, it is imperative that divers be specially trained in deep diving and/or technical diving.

Classes will teach you to recognize symptoms of narcosis and proper decompression procedures when doing deep or repetitive deep dives. Remember, emergency facilities in PNG are limited. Know your limits and don't push your luck when it comes to depth.

Diving in Papua New Guinea

BOB HALSTEAD

PNG's reefs are unique because they are the only reefs close to the heart of the Indo-Pacific not subject to degradation by the pressures of a massive human population.

The 40,000 sq km (15,400 sq miles) of coral reef support virtually no commercial fisheries and a coastal population of only about 3 million people.

The seas that contain the Philippine Islands, the Indonesian archipelago and PNG are recognized as having the greatest marine biodiversity in the world. Estimates indicate that PNG may have up to twice as many marine species as the Red Sea and up to five times as many as the Caribbean. This coral wonderland means an almost endless variety of dive sites.

Barrier reefs are rimmed by coral walls that plunge steeply to the abyss. Inside the barrier are lagoons sheltered from ocean swells, supporting shallow coral gardens and patch reefs. Hundreds of tiny coral islands dot the lagoons and, along the shore, vast stretches of mangroves provide vital nursery areas.

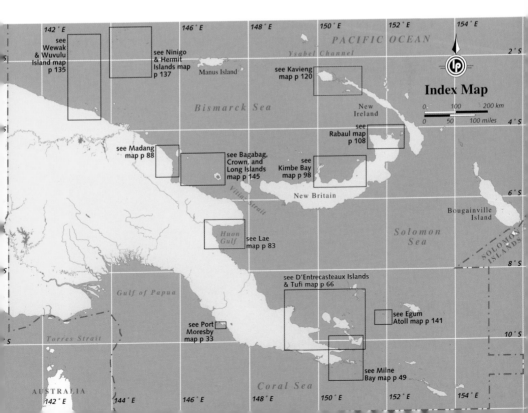

Index Map

PACIFIC OCEAN

see Wewak & Wuvulu Island map p 135

see Ninigo & Hermit Islands map p 137

Manus Island

Ysabel Channel

see Kavieng map p 120

New Ireland

Bismarck Sea

0   100   200 km
0   50   100 miles

see Madang map p 88

see Bagabag, Crown, and Long Islands map p 145

see Kimbe Bay map p 98

see Rabaul map p 108

Vitiaz Strait

New Britain

Bougainville Island

Huon Gulf

see Lae map p 83

Solomon Sea

SOLOMON ISLANDS

see D'Entrecasteaux Islands & Tufi map p 66

Gulf of Papua

see Port Moresby map p 33

see Egum Atoll map p 141

Torres Strait

see Milne Bay map p 49

Coral Sea

AUSTRALIA

PNG also has classic coral atolls where tidal waters rich in plankton rush in and out of the passes twice a day and support dazzling displays of abundant life. Spicing up all of this are some magnificent wrecks—of ships, aircraft and even submarines, mainly but not entirely from WWII.

PNG's many dive tour operators are spread throughout the various centers and are careful to preserve reef quality by ensuring that responsible anchoring procedures or moorings are used. This limits the number of divers on individual reefs and allows reefs to recover after any damage.

Undoubtedly pressures to increase exploitation of coral reef resources are growing. Present threats to the health of PNG's coral reefs include irresponsible logging that causes run-off to smother the reefs. The promotion of the shark finning industry, which can devastate reefs by removing an animal essential for their good health has, so far, been kept at bay.

Certification

All diving operators in PNG have internationally qualified instructors—NAUI and PADI—but live-aboard dive boats do not generally offer basic instruction. Some live-aboards do offer Nitrox and Rebreather courses to experienced divers.

Snorkeling in PNG

Snorkeling in PNG can be a real treat. Many dive boats and live-aboards moor in shallow water just above the reeftops. Fish life can be quite active around these moorings and the corals are usually healthy along the drop-off rims. Snorkeling the seamounts in the rich, blue water in Kimbe Bay can be particularly rewarding. Sites along fringing reefs can also be good for shore-based snorkeling.

Many shallow, historical remnants in PNG waters are great for snorkeling. One of the best sites holds two Japanese tanks that rest in only 4m, near the northern tip of Duke of York Island. The tanks are not armed and a sunken barge lies nearby so it is assumed the tanks sank while being transported. The tanks are upright, one behind the other, and present a surreal sight.

Current changes can come up quickly, so do not snorkel alone and make sure a proper pick-up boat is available to get you in case you are carried off.

BOB HALSTEAD

Shore-based operators generally have scuba and snorkeling gear for rent. Depending on the operation, introductory certification courses are available, but call ahead to determine the instructor and course availability. The greatest variety of instruction is found around the Port Moresby area, where many of the locals get certified.

It is probably more economical and generally recommended that you get initial certification at home prior to coming to PNG for holiday, as instruction here can get expensive.

Most resorts also offer snorkeling as well as scuba trips.

Dive Site Icons

The symbols at the beginning of the dive site descriptions provide a quick summary of some of the following characteristics present at the site:

 Good snorkeling or free-diving site.

 Remains or partial remains of a wreck can be seen at this site.

 Sheer wall or drop-off.

 Deep dive. Features of this dive occur in water deeper than 27m (90ft).

 Strong currents may be encountered at this site.

 Strong surge (the horizontal movement of water caused by waves) may be encountered at this site.

 Drift dive. Because of strong currents and/or difficulty in anchoring, a drift dive is recommended at this site.

 Beach/shore dive. This site can be accessed from shore.

 Poor visibility. The site often has visibility of less than 8m (25ft).

 Caves are a prominent feature of this site. Only experienced cave divers should explore inner cave areas.

Depth Range

The depth range indicated in each dive site summary gives the actual depth of the reef or wreck on the site. PNG has many deep dive sites with reefs that extend right up to the surface. Many interesting creatures can be found in these extreme shallows. "0" depth indicates that the reef or wreck reaches the surface or extends out of the water. "40m (130ft) plus" depth indicates that the site goes deeper than 40m (130ft), which is the maximum depth for sport diving. Be appropriately cautious on these dives to not sink below your intended maximum depth.

Pisces Rating System for Dives & Divers

The dive sites in this book are rated according to the following diver skill level rating system. These are not absolute ratings but apply to divers at a particular time, diving at a particular place. For instance, someone unfamiliar with prevailing conditions might be considered a novice diver at one dive area, but an intermediate diver at another, more familiar location.

Novice: A novice diver generally fits the following profile:
◆ basic scuba certification from an internationally recognized certifying agency
◆ dives infrequently (less than one trip a year)
◆ logged fewer than 25 total dives
◆ dives no deeper than 18m (60ft)
◆ little or no experience diving in similar waters and conditions
* A novice diver should be accompanied by an instructor, divemaster or advanced diver on all dives

Intermediate: An intermediate diver generally fits the following profile:
◆ may have participated in some form of continuing diver education
◆ logged between 25 and 100 dives
◆ dives no deeper than 40m (130ft)
◆ has been diving within the last six months in similar waters and conditions

Advanced: An advanced diver generally fits the following profile:
◆ advanced certification
◆ has been diving for more than 2 years; logged over 100 dives
◆ has been diving within the last six months in similar waters and conditions

Regardless of skill level, you should be in good physical condition and know your limitations. If you are uncertain as to your own level of expertise, ask the advice of a local dive instructor. He or she is best qualified to assess your abilities based on the prevailing dive conditions at any given site. Ultimately you must decide if you are capable of making a particular dive, depending on your level of training, recent experience, and physical condition, as well as water conditions at the site. Remember that water conditions can change at any time, even during a dive.

Port Moresby Dive Sites

Port Moresby, the nation's capital, is normally the visiting diver's first glimpse at the mysterious land of PNG. The view immediately holds great promise.

Flying in, you'll see the iridescent ribbon of the Papuan Barrier Reef, clearly visible just before landing. Swells from the Coral Sea break in lines of white foam along the outer edges, and dark canyons cut the ribbon at Basilisk Passage and outside Bootless Inlet. These reef passes, just a few kilometers offshore, are the most popular areas for divers, offering protection from the surf, exciting big fish encounters and the magnificent coral of outer barrier reefs.

Port Moresby itself is the main business and political center of the country and is a busy place but not congested. Most visitors note the shanty towns along the seashore and the barbed wire on the compounds, businesses and homes. This is a city of haves and have-nots and the wire, guards and dogs make sure the two remain separate.

Weather Conditions

WIND: The southeast trade winds from May through November can reach 25 knots, countered by strong land breezes from the mountains behind Port Moresby. Early morning, the water is often calm all the way out to the barrier reef. From January through April winds swing unpredictably between northwest and southwest, with periodic strong rain squalls called *Gubas*.

RAIN: There is very little rainfall in Port Moresby during the southeast season. Even in the rainy season, December through April, average rainfall is much less than most coastal regions of PNG.

WATER TEMPERATURE: Varies from average lows of 25°C (77°F) during July/August up to average highs of 28°C (82°F) during January/February. Occasionally temperatures fall to 24°C (75°F) or rise to 29°C (84°F).

Spinner and bottlenose dolphins follow the *Solatai* out to Port Morseby dive sites.

As such, it is not the safest city in the world but does have a certain charm, and places like the National Museum offer a fascinating glimpse of the country and its incredible cultural diversity.

Port Moresby Diving

Port Moresby has probably the best diving of any capital city in the world. Several islands inside the lagoon offer sheltered anchorages in windy conditions and good diving for those interested in seeking unusual small animals.

Coral growth and marine life are excellent. The only negative is that visibility is sometimes reduced when murky water from the bays and lagoon washes out over the outer reef. If seas are calm, and dives planned on incoming tides, the visibility is over 30m (98ft).

Several wrecks are dived, from Bootless Inlet Marina (southeast of Port Moresby) and Loloata Island Resort. Many derelict vessels were sunk deliberately, but there are also some aircraft remains, including a fine example of an A-20 Havoc.

Port Moresby Dive Sites	Good Snorkeling	Novice	Intermediate	Advanced
1 The Finger	●		●	
2 The Beacon	●		●	
3 *New Marine & Kukipi*		●		
4 Fisherman's Island Area	●		●	
5 Local Island & Bottle Dump		●	●	
6 Sunken Barrier			●	
7 Suzie's Bommie			●	
8 Baldwin's Bommie	●		●	
9 Horseshoe Reef	●	●		
10 *Pacific Gas (Nanayo Maru)*				●
11 Patch Reefs	●		●	
12 Bootless Inlet	●	●		
13 Papuan Barrier Reef	●		●	
14 Eastern Fields	●			●

The ocean view from the front porch of the Loloata Island Resort.

A 10-hour cruise from Port Moresby brings you to Eastern Fields, one of the most magnificent of all Coral Sea reefs. Few people visit here as there is really no land mass. Under the sea you can expect fantastically clear water, superb coral formations and encounters with sharks and other big fish. This is a live-aboard destination and the best time to dive it is in March to May and November to January.

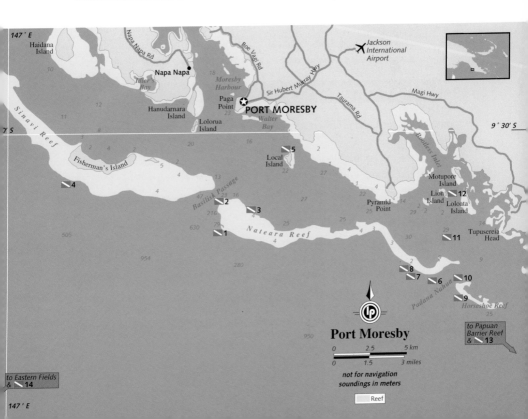

1 The Finger

The most popular site reached from Port Moresby is The Finger, situated just outside the main entrance in the barrier reef known as Basilisk Passage. Small speedboats can reach the site in 30-40 minutes. A beacon marks the entrance to the eastern reef. The Finger is a descending coral ridge on a sand slope that juts out from the main reef about 2km past the beacon.

The barrier reef here drops deep into the Coral Sea and offers a good chance to see larger pelagic fish. Hammerhead and

Location: Basilisk Passage, outer barrier

Depth Range: 5-40m (16-130ft) plus

Access: Boat

Expertise Rating: Intermediate

grey reef sharks are often encountered, along with schools of fish and occasional manta rays. In calm weather, boats can anchor in relatively shallow water on top of the reef and divers can either opt to snorkel, do a shallow dive, or follow the reef down to deeper waters.

This site is, however, exposed to the southeast trade winds and is often inaccessible, particularly later in the day. During the southeast season, which runs from about May through November, diving is generally better in the morning when land breezes counter the trade winds and keep the seas calm.

A curious manta ray makes a shallow pass.

2 The Beacon

Ocean swells can be a problem outside the reef, but there are several partially sheltered sites in Basilisk Passage. These sites are generally known as The Beacon.

Tidal currents through the passage can be formidable but are predictable with tide tables; usually the best time to dive is at the end of the incoming tide. Drift dives are also possible through the passage but these should only be attempted with an incoming current.

The eastern side of the passage is the most scenic with a vertical cliff face starting in shallow water (5m). Many cracks, overhangs and swim-throughs

Location: Basilisk Passage, outer barrier

Depth Range: 5-40m (16-130ft) plus

Access: Boat

Expertise Rating: Intermediate

are home to plenty of fish and occasional sea fans and whips. Sea snakes are regularly encountered but rarely show interest in divers.

3 New Marine & Kukipi

On the inner slope of the barrier reef about 2km inside the eastern side of Basilisk Passage rests a pair of wrecks

Location: Inside Basilisk Passage

Depth Range: 5-23m (16-76ft)

Access: Boat

Expertise Rating: Novice

Marine life abounds on the *New Marine*.

sunk by local divers. The 30m-long fishing trawler *New Marine* and the smaller *Kukipi* lie side-by-side, facing opposite directions, with the deepest part of the wrecks at 23m.

They are well-sheltered by the reef and offer diving when conditions are unsuitable elsewhere. Soft corals have grown on the wrecks, along with a healthy population of fish life, including a resident school of batfish.

4 Fisherman's Island Area

Fisherman's Island, on the barrier reef west of Basilisk Passage, is a popular weekend picnic spot for local boat owners. The anchorage is good but the dive sites are on the seaward side of the island. Small boats can cross over the reeftop at high tide in calm conditions, and anchor on the edge of an impressive drop-off that falls vertically for the first 30m and then transforms into sand slope.

Coral life is good, and leopard sharks are often seen resting on the sand at the base of the drop-off. You can access several different sites, including **Owen Stanleys**, which is rather different than the others because of its scenic, undulating coral formations on the reeftop that slope down to the deeper drop-off.

Location: Outer barrier reef near Fisherman's Island

Depth Range: 5-40m (16-130ft) plus

Access: Boat

Expertise Rating: Intermediate

Farther west several other dive sites have good fish life and shark action but are seldom blessed with visibility as good as Basilisk Passage and Fisherman's Island.

At **Lagamara** on the eastern side of Haidana Passage, the reef wall is dramatically sculptured with cracks and overhangs, swim-throughs and some

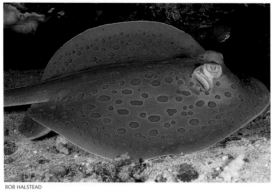

Bluespotted stingrays hang out on the sandy bottom.

isolated coral towers. Eagle rays are regularly seen at this site.

Bava 98 has some of the best shark action near Port Moresby, along with the drop-off at **Idihi Island**. These are the farthest dive sites visited by local divers from Port Moresby ,and take about 50 minutes to reach by small speedboat.

5 Local Island & Bottle Dump

Local Island provides excellent shelter and anchorage in the southeast season though the diving is again rather poor at the anchorage.

However, scattered outcrops of coral may be found on the silty bottom and have surprisingly healthy marine life. The eastern side of the island has a well-formed coral reef that may be dived in the northwest season.

Even though Port Moresby Harbour has little to offer divers due to the poor visibility, you may want to check out the **Bottle Dump**. At this site, local divers found intact glass bottles, which serve as historical evidence of where Port Moresby's early European inhabitants dumped their rubbish.

Location: In lagoon east of entrance to Port Moresby Harbour

Depth Range: 0-20m (0-66ft)

Access: Boat/Shore

Expertise Rating: Novice/Intermediate

A diver checks out the glass bottles that were left as garbage by early PNG residents.

Day Trips from Bootless Inlet

The marina at Bootless Inlet is only a 15-minute drive southeast from the Port Moresby Airport, about the same time it takes to drive to the downtown harbor. The outer barrier reef is only 8km away from the marina where a passage, Padana Nahua, separates the Sunken Barrier from Horseshoe Reef. The nice thing about diving here is that local dive boat operators and the marina management are constantly exploring new sites. Ask if there are any newly discovered hot spots, especially along the southern outer barrier reef.

The bridge of the *Pacific Gas*, which was sunk as an artificial reef in Padana Nahua passage.

6 Sunken Barrier

The Sunken Barrier is the eastern section of the reef starting at Basilisk Passage. It is called "sunken" because the reeftop is under deeper water, averaging 4m, and waves rarely break on it. This results in better coral growth than on other parts of the barrier. The disadvantage is that the reef provides no shelter and can also experience stronger currents. But in calm conditions, and at times of modest currents, the Sunken Barrier offers some excellent dive sites.

The most dramatic of these is the **Big Drop,** right at the southeastern tip of the reef. A steep drop-off starts in 5m and falls to a lip at 30m where it forms an undercut vertical cliff, apparently falling for more than 100m before sloping deep into the Coral Sea. At 40m, several large sea fans are suspended over the abyss and are visited by silvertip and hammerhead sharks. Like most parts of the outer barrier reef, even if surface waters are murky, at 40m the water is usually clear.

Location: Outer reef west of Padana Nahua passage

Depth Range: 5-40m (16-130ft) plus

Access: Boat

Expertise Rating: Intermediate

Hammerhead sharks frequent the Big Drop.

7 Suzie's Bommie

A top dive site on the sunken barrier is **Suzie's Bommie** where a deep coral tower just off the wall rises to about 12m below the surface. This is a favorite spot for visiting photographers to create fantastic macro images.

The channel between the bommie and the wall bottoms out at about 30m and this is one of the sites where the unusual and extremely tiny pygmy seahorses are found on *muricella* gorgonian sea fans. Divers without "young eyes" might want to bring a magnifying glass to help spot these miniature invertebrates. Fish life in this little channel

Location: Outer reef west of Padana Nahua passage

Depth Range: 5-40m (16-130ft) plus

Access: Boat

Expertise Rating: Intermediate

can be good with large groupers and Napoleon wrasses swimming nearby.

The most spectacular part of this dive is at the top of the bommie, where you'll see a huge, resident school of mixed sweetlips and batfish. These fish make for some very colorful photographs.

Many fish also gather along the sides of this tiny pinnacle and cluster around stands of tubastrea corals. The mooring for Suzie's is on the other side of the saddle, on a different, shallower bommie. Keep an eye out for the crocodilefish that are often seen swimming around this mount.

Fusiliers school with sweetlips atop Suzies.

Pygmy Seahorses

The pygmy seahorse (*Hippocampus bargibanti*), an amazingly tiny creature just found and regularly photographed in the last few years, is a must-find for macrophotographers to add to their portfolios. Although it has been found now in some places in Indonesia and off Australia's Great Barrier Reef, the pygmy seems to be most prolific along PNG reefs.

Naturalist divemasters near Port Moresby have identified the sites with the sea fans that the pygmies seem to favor. It truly helps to have someone along who knows what to look for. Even if you know what a *Muricella* gorgonian is, the seahorses are only 2cm (.8 inch) high.

They cling to the fan with strong tails and camouflage using small bumps on their bodies that mimic polyps. They are notoriously shy. Many divers bring magnifying glasses and pointers to find these mini-seahorses.

Reports verify regular pygmy sightings at at least four sites in Kimbe, and along the outer Horseshoe Reef of Loloata. But be prepared to hunt for a while for these hard-to-spot creatures. They tend to like cooler water and some current, so you may have to dive to 30m or more.

8 Baldwin's Bommie

This is another dive where the mooring is on a different reef than the actual dive site.

Named as a favorite of Kevin Baldwin, owner of the dive boat *Tiata*, which is based in Bootless Bay, the dive entails swimming along a longer, loaf-shaped reef, highlighted by various hard corals and invertebrates.

Sea snakes are often seen grazing in the area, looking for small critters to

Location: Outer reef

Depth Range: 6-40m (20-130ft) plus

Access: Boat

Expertise Rating: Intermediate

munch on. Watching them swim with their paddle tail is a fascinating sight.

Following the reef you will come to a saddle that dips down to 27m and then

BOB HALSTEAD

Longnose hawkfish.

slopes. There is a very large *muricella* coral fan here with a resident longnose hawkfish. Divemasters also check this fan periodically for pygmy seahorses when the cooling upwellings are prevalent.

Baldwin's Reef is on the other side of the saddle and when the current is running, it is a great fishwatching place. Swirls of fusiliers swarm the reeftop and surgeonfish, sweetlips and other schooling fish bring the reef to life. Take a leisurely swim back to the boat, studying the reeftop life while making a safety decompression stop.

9 Horseshoe Reef

Horseshoe Reef is one of the most popular dive sites from Bootless Inlet because it offers a variety of good dives protected by the reef in the southeast season. The **End Bommie** is an exceptional site with sea fans, excellent hard and soft corals and prolific fish life.

Boats should anchor on top of Horseshoe Reef at its western end, in 4m. Farther west along the edge of a vertical wall, you'll meet a saddle in the reef at 20m, which then rises to the **End Bommie** itself.

The bommie is easily circumnavigated to find the side with most fish. The fish life is best at incoming tide, but at slack tide sea fans and other invertebrates keep the dive interesting. Resident lacy scorpionfish make this site a big draw for fish photographers. Baby whitetip reef sharks like to rest under the plate corals on top of the Bommie.

Location: Outer barrier reef east of Padana Nahua passage

Depth Range: 3-40m (10-130ft) plus

Access: Boat

Expertise Rating: Novice

The reef slopes away to deep water and is often visited by larger sharks. On the south side of the saddle a large field of sand forms an amphitheater defined by a

BOB HALSTEAD

This rare pink rhinopias was found on the End Bommie.

deep ribbon reef and a reef wall with several channels cutting into it. Near the mooring a large expanse of sea anemones has literally hundreds of resident clownfish. This is a nice spot to do a safety decompression stop while watching the fish action.

In all, it is a lovely and lively site and, when the water is clear, it is one of the best in the Port Moresby area.

Near the midpoint of the sheltered side of Horseshoe Reef three sunken boats create an artificial reef. The government trawler *Parama* and the workboat *Jade* were the first boats deliberately sunk in PNG. These two boats were constructed with wood and not much remains of them today.

However, a 25m steel fishing trawler, the *Pai*, was also sunk in an upright position with all its fishing masts intact. This is a fascinating dive, attracting a healthy population of fish and adorned with soft corals. The wheelhouse is home to a school of copper sweepers that glisten as sunlight shines through the many win-

BOB HALSTEAD
The *Pai* is a favorite wreck dive, night or day.

dows, and giant puffer has taken up residence atop the ship.

This is a particularly good night dive with many large, sleeping coral trout. Wobbegong sharks are usually in the area, although their effective camouflage makes them hard to spot. This area has also been visited by manta rays, young hammerhead sharks and even whale sharks. The wreck lies on a sand slope with nearby coral patches, its bow in the deepest part at 27m.

TIM ROCK

A large school of copper sweepers makes the *Pai* wheelhouse home.

10 *Pacific Gas (Nanayo Maru)*

This upright ship is one of the area's best attractions, combining wreck and reef diving in one. The *Nanayo Maru*, commonly known as the *Pacific Gas*, was sunk in 1986 to create an artificial reef. The 65m-long liquid gas carrier had its huge gas tanks removed before it sunk upright, with its bow at 14m and the pro-

Location: 1km north of Horseshoe Reef

Depth Range: 14-43m (46-141ft)

Access: Boat

Expertise Rating: Advanced

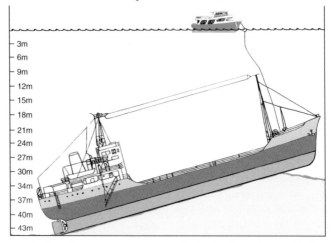

- 3m
- 6m
- 9m
- 12m
- 15m
- 18m
- 21m
- 24m
- 27m
- 30m
- 34m
- 37m
- 40m
- 43m

Dive boats anchor on a mooring line attached to the bow of the *Pacific Gas*.

peller at 43m. Positioned to take advantage of the tidal flow in and out of the Padana Nahua passage, the wreck quickly gained beautiful growths of soft corals and masses of fish life.

TIM ROCK
The entire wreck is alive with coral and fish life.

Follow the mooring line down to the bow and then swim along the open hold to the deeper portions of the ship. The bridge sits on top of the accommodations and the engine room at the stern, both of which are accessible to careful divers. The bridge is generally surrounded by a large school of yellow-tailed, robust fusiliers that sometimes move into the bridge, filling it with color. The sea fans around the deck area provide hiding places for ornate ghost pipefish during certain times of the year. The bow has a resident population of lionfish who nip at the baitfish. Giant grouper are sometimes seen near a cleaning station on the bow mast.

11 Patch Reefs

Several patch reefs such as **South Patch** and **Quayle's Reef** are scattered in the lagoon out of Bootless Inlet and are colorful, healthy reefs with plenty of marine life. They are relatively shallow on top, averaging 6m and sloping away to 30 or 40m. They are often favored for night diving.

Look for the unusual candelabra corals at Quayle's Reef. There are also stands of red sea whips and some nice collections of hard corals harboring many juvenile fish. Cuttlefish are also found at Quayle's.

South Patch is a real haven for hard and soft corals with a couple of immense table corals, large enough for a diver to get under and look out. A wall of fluffy leather coral falls down near the mooring, where anemones, nudibranchs and some stunning tunicate colonies dot the landscape.

Miku's is another new site in this group. It has sea whips with resident whip gobies and some nice stands of let-

Location: In lagoon between Bootless Inlet and outer barrier reef

Depth Range: 5-30m (16-100ft) plus

Access: Boat

Expertise Rating: Intermediate

Colorful tunicate colonies bloom along the sloping walls of the reef.

tuce corals and sea fans. Some very cooperative saddleback anemonefish can be found at the reeftop.

12 Bootless Inlet

Close to shore and a few minutes' boat ride from the Bootless Inlet Marina

Location: Entrance to Bootless Inlet

Depth Range: 0-30m (0-100ft) plus

Access: Boat

Expertise Rating: Novice

BOB HALSTEAD

Loloata with the mainland in the background.

(known as Tahira Marina) are three islands: **Lion Island**, which is uninhabited, **Motupore Island**, which has a biological research station run by the University of PNG, and the third, **Loloata Island**, the home of Loloata Island Resort.

Loloata Island has some nice snorkeling sites and some interesting creatures live in the seagrasses near the long Loloata Dock. From October through February a huge school of baitfish appear, making the water almost black with fish. It is a wonderful place to snorkel or dive at high tide.

Chocolate sea stars and anemones decorate the sea floor at Lion Island.

Loloata also features a WWII aircraft wreck, the **Boston A20 Havoc**. The wreck was found by local scientists doing marine biology research on sea cucumbers. Resting south of the island in 18m of silty water in a reef hollow, the aircraft is in good condition and is an interesting dive for aircraft enthusiasts. Only the nose gunner's section was dislodged from the aircraft when it ditched, and this can be found on the silty bottom 30m or so behind the tail.

Lion Island may be dived even in the very worst weather when the outer reefs

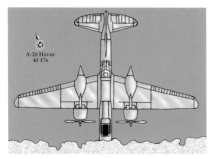

The Boston Havoc rests, noseless, in 18m.

become inaccessible. Although the visibility rarely exceeds 15m (and is often less), the reef surrounding the island, particularly on its southern side, is rich with life.

The **Sea Grass Beds** north of the beach site at Lion Island have become a muck diver's dream, with many small invertebrates and unusual fish. Depths here range from 2 to 17m before the bottom becomes silty. Look for large and small anemones with saddleback and two-stripe anemonefish. A myriad of cleaning stations hold lots of barber pole, snow-capped and short-capped shrimp. Various pipefish slink through the grasses and the whole area is punctuated by chocolate chip sea stars. Squid like to hang around the mooring buoy.

Four boats have been sunk near the island. One is a tugboat. The *Tuart* in

Pipefish slink in and out of sea grass.

15m—which was, ironically, used to tow the *Parama* when it was sunk—is on the south side. A fishing trawler, the **New Marine #6**, resting at 20m on the eastern side, also boasts a wall with significant growths of black coral. Look for large puffers, lionfish and soft coral crabs on this ship. A small coastal barge, the *Sir Godfrey* rests in 15m at the northern end. Nearby in shallow water the ferrocement yacht *Lady Jules* sits with nice soft coral growths on its bow.

Muck Diving, A PNG Specialty

Want to know where to find many of the weird and unusual creatures that you see in the books about PNG's sea life?

Sea grass beds and mangroves with only sparse coral growth, where the visibility may not be as sparkling as the off-shore reefs, are usually areas most divers avoid. But, be forewarned, in PNG these dives—aptly named "muck dives"—can become addictive.

The sheltered reefs and bays are increasingly popular with divers. Not only is the diving easier (without waves and currents), and shallower (allowing longer bottom times), these areas are home to a multitude of unusual and exotic marine creatures found nowhere else.

Photographers will find abundant opportunities for brilliant marine life shots. Muck diving

areas harbor sea horses, juvenile batfish, warty frogfish, banded snake eels, anemones, their residents, and juvenile striped catfish, which are often seen massed in tight "balls."

Don't let first impressions of the often poorly developed reefs that survive in these areas, or the wharves and wrecks close to shore, get the best of you. The muck is worth a much closer look.

Banded snake eel

13 Papuan Barrier Reef

To the southeast along the Papuan Barrier towards Round Point are many good, but only occasionally visited, dive sites. When the weather is favorable and longer boat trips from Bootless Inlet are possible this area is well worth diving.

The barrier reef runs parallel to the coast about 5km offshore for nearly 40km, and is cut with about 10 passes, including the **Pumpkin Patch**, **Pinnacles**, **PJ Pass** and **Sandy Passage**.

One newly named site, **Nadine's Passage**, is particularly beautiful, with its east side landscaped with large sea fans, big soft corals and fields of red sea whips. Manta rays have been seen feeding here on the incoming tide, and the shallow reeftop above the channel is a good place to look for reef sharks and sea turtles. The rubbly areas also produce some unusual nudibranchs.

Location: Outer Barrier reef east of Bootless Inlet

Depth Range: 5-40m (16-130ft) plus

Access: Boat

Expertise Rating: Intermediate

BOB HALSTEAD

14 Eastern Fields

Just a 10-hour cruise southwest of Port Moresby lies the magnificent Eastern Fields, a Coral Sea reef system boasting virtually untouched diving and fantastic visibility, often reaching 50m. It is possible to enter the reef-formed lagoon for secure anchorage. You can dive the bommies in the lagoon, the passes and outer walls.

Big sharks including scalloped hammerheads, silvertips and even tiger and great hammerheads are regularly seen, together with schools of pelagic and reef fish. Being the most northerly of the Coral Sea reefs, Eastern Fields do not suffer the devastating effects of cyclones that occasionally damage reefs farther south.

Carl's Ultimate was named after Carl Roessler, one of the world's most-traveled divers. He declared the site the best he had ever encountered for its combination of prolific hard and soft coral growths and constant big fish action. Don't miss the series of tunnels at one end of the reef, filled with soft corals and buzzing with trevally.

Location: 167km (90 nautical miles) southwest of Port Moresby

Depth Range: 5-40m (16-130ft) plus

Access: Live-aboard

Expertise Rating: Advanced

Craig's Ultimate was named for Craig De Wit, operator of the live-aboard *Golden Dawn*, which specializes in trips to Eastern Fields. Craig's is a wonderfully sculptured reef decorated with soft corals and regularly visited by both scalloped and great hammerhead sharks. Diving the Coral Sea is not for the faint-hearted.

In addition to the big animal encounters, more sites are being discovered with a surprising array of exotic macro critters including the blue ribbon eel, a favorite photographic subject.

The remote Eastern Fields, offshore in the Coral Sea, boasts pristine walls and incredible visibility.

Milne Bay Dive Sites

To divers, Milne Bay may be best known as the place where muck diving went from a diversion to an art. Small and unusual creatures flourish here. This province of scattered islands and reef systems is the easternmost end of the Papuan mainland.

Development isn't what it used to be in the Milne Bay Province. Samarai Island was once the center of trade and commerce for the region, but nowadays this little ghost town reflects the quiet pace of the entire area. Once a flourishing trade center dating back many centuries, it has now fallen off the trade routes—good for visitors wanting to see fewer tourists. However, local fisheries are hoping to see a revival of trade to help the economy here.

BOB HALSTEAD

Friendly villagers wave hello at this East Cape guesthouse.

Weather Conditions

WIND: Southeast trade winds blow from May through November. December to April (cyclone season in the Coral Sea) is generally calm with short—but strong—blows from the northwest or southwest.

RAIN: Rainfall in Milne Bay is difficult to predict. Statistically the wettest months are May, August and September; however, rainfall tends to be localized, and some years are quite dry.

WATER TEMPERATURE: Varies from average lows of 26°C (79°F) during June/July up to average highs of 28°C (82°F) during January/February. Occasionally temperatures fall to 25°C (77°F) or rise to 30°C (86°F).

Milne Bay Province and its many islands (officially 435, but there are many more) can't be described in a couple of simple sentences. The spine of PNG—the Owen Stanley Range—meets the sea here. Many seaside villages line the shoreline, but not a lot of people live in the mountains and foothills. Some islands are rugged and mountainous with only coastal villages while others are small, flat and sandy. Weather can be erratic and unpredictable. Spectacular lightning storms illuminate the sky when they roll out of the mountains.

Milne Bay Diving

In the past, Milne Bay was best known as the site of a bloody WWII battle, but this is rapidly changing to a much more pleasant association: the starting point for some of the most wonderful diving in the Indo-Pacific. Although the bay itself does not have much to offer divers, Milne Bay Province has more reefs and islands than any other province in PNG.

Reefs grow right up to the shoreline and, with plenty of variety, competition for space among corals is intense, making for some beautiful reef structures. The reefs are typically mixtures of hard and soft corals, with sea fans and sea whips decorating reef slopes and inhabited by a bewildering profusion of marine life.

Milne Bay Dive Sites	Good Snorkeling	Novice	Intermediate	Advanced
15 Muscoota	●	●		
16 Sullivan's Patches	●		●	
17 East Cape	●		●	
18 Banana Bommie	●		●	
19 North Coast	●	●		
20 Kathy's Corner	●	●		
21 Deacon's Reef & Dinah's Beach	●	●		
22 Nuakata Island to Basilaki Island	●			●
23 Peer's Reef	●			●
24 Boirama Reef	●			●
25 Gallows Reef	●		●	
26 Doubilet Reef & Basilaki Island				●
27 P38 Lightning Aircraft Wreck			●	
28 China Strait & Samarai				●
29 Daisy's Drop-Off				●
30 President Grant	●		●	
31 Sawa Sawaga				●
32 Giants at Home	●		●	

150° 30' E

151° E

Duchess Island

Awaiara Bay

S   10° S

478   *Sewa Bay*
2

Normanby Island

Goschen Strait

• Bunama

Puni Puni
Point   85   Cape Ventenat
            706
        32   Hulana
             Cape   450
                                      Basilisk Point   East   **17** Boia Boia Waga Island
        Bentley Bay   **21**   **19**   Cape   **23**   **25**
rles Abel Hwy   **20**   Meimciara   **18** Nuakata   261
• **Alotau**   Island 36   Island **24** *Gallows
                                                                                                   Reef*
urney
irport   59   • Ahioma   81   **22**   324
                                              95   4
Aleford Island   **16**   2
2   297   4
scovery Bay 382   2   o Blakeney
    15   *Milne Bay*   540   2   12   Island

• Wagawaga   545   **26**

30° S   531   2   10° 30' S

                                 34   8   5   *Engineer Group*
                    China Strait   **27**   101
             28   Sarabi   Sideia   Basilaki Island   5
                       Island   Island   160
             Samarai   38
             Island   **31**   Rogeia   Connor Island 129
             Island   **32**   18
                                       Doini
             40   Island   11
rumer   17
sland 8
    7   16   11   *Siga Island*
                                                                             11
13   Dunoulin Island
        12   22   11
             12   14   **29** Wari Island 56
                       16

S   13   11° S
             457

                       Coral   783   *Uluma   10 Imbert Island
             lp   *Sea*   Reef*
                                   30

Milne Bay
0   10   20 km
0   5   10 miles
not for navigation
soundings in meters
  Reef

150° 30' E

151° E

If you're looking for Mr. Big, the denizens of the deep will not disappoint. With big shoals nearby, the higher end of the food chain is well-represented: hammerheads and other sharks swim along the drop-offs, manta rays and even whale sharks make regular visits.

In other areas, sheltered, scattered coral and sea grass beds are home to a multitude of unusual creatures, including ghost pipefish, panda clownfish, sea moths and mantis shrimp. The diversity of marine life in Milne Bay Province is simply unrivalled.

The islands and reefs near East Cape and Nuakata Island at the mouth of the bay, the north coast, and the waters surrounding the volcanic D'Entrecasteaux Islands are the main areas regularly dived, but many more await exploration.

The provincial capital of Alotau is on the north shore of Milne Bay. Since most of the best diving begins a long boat ride away at the mouth of Milne Bay near East Cape, attempting day dives from Alotau is not the best way to dive the province. However, a couple of dives worth mentioning, the *Muscoota* and Sullivan's Patches, are not far from Alotau.

Lionfish hunting at Kathy's Corner.

15 *Muscoota*

In Discovery Bay, on the south side of Milne Bay opposite Alotau, lies the wreck of the *Muscoota*, once a proud four-masted, iron-hulled sailing clipper originally called the *Buckingham*.

During WWII the ship was converted to a coal refueling barge with a giant sliding crane over the hull. When she sprang a leak she was towed into Discovery Bay, where she sank with the tip of her bow sticking out of the water near the beach, and her rudder in 24m.

The bow is still visible above the surface, but the crane recently collapsed over the stern. The wreck gained prolific growths of soft corals, encrusting sponges and leaf oysters. Schools of fish swim among the huge girders of the crane and a wobbegong shark is often found resting on the deck.

The wreck is historically interesting and coal can be seen in the open holds; however, the inside compartments are badly silted. The visibility is often poor but can reach 18m in good conditions.

For macro photography and weird marine creatures this is a terrific dive. Seahorses, anemonefish, ghost pipefish,

Location: Discovery Bay

Depth Range: 0-24m (0-79ft)

Access: Boat or shore

Expertise Rating: Novice

flying gurnards, frogfish, ribbon and shrimp gobies, colorful fire urchins, nudibranchs, shells of all descriptions and a host of other gems live in the sea grass and sand surrounding the wreck. The local villagers have built a guest house near the wreck and welcome visitors.

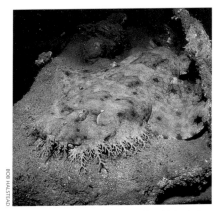

A wobbegong shark rests on the ship's deck.

Lionfish on the *Muscoota's* funnel.

16 Sullivan's Patches

Sullivan's Patches consist of two sausage-shaped reefs at right angles to one another. In the 1980s the reef was devastated by an outbreak of crown-of-thorns sea stars, but now the patches have excellent coral cover of both hard and soft corals and are alive with many species of tropical reef fish—good evidence of the rejuvenating ability of coral reefs.

The reefs, which rise to 6m, are about 6km offshore and are usually blessed with clear water. Sharks and manta rays are occasionally seen. Take care not to damage the coral by anchoring on the

Location: In Milne Bay 30km east of Alotau

Depth Range: 6-40m (20-130ft) plus

Access: Boat

Expertise Rating: Intermediate

reef. Use sand patches on the northern side of the westerly reef, and near the eastern tip of the easterly reef, where a saddle leads to an isolated bommie.

17 East Cape

The East Cape, the eastern tip of New Guinea, and the north shore west of the Cape, have some excellent dive sites. Just off the Cape are two lovely islands, **Mei Mei'ara** and **Boia Boia Waga**. Drop-offs on their northern sides plunge steeply from shallow depths to several hundred meters. On their southern sides you'll find incredibly rich scattered coral, fed by currents that surge around the Cape.

The mostly unpredictable currents can make diving difficult. However, for most of the year, if the sites and times are selected carefully, currents are easily managed and the dives are wonderful.

Location: Northeast tip of Milne Bay

Depth Range: 0-40m (0-130ft) plus

Access: Live-aboard

Expertise Rating: Intermediate

Enormous schools of fish parade along the reef fronts. Visibility in the area is often over 30m, but heavy rainfall can reduce surface visibility. Deeper down the walls you'll find the visibility dramatically improves.

Around November/December, the plankton bloom sometimes attracts manta rays and whale sharks. Large mantas swim together in the channel between the islands. Minke whales, pilot whales and even killer whales (orcas) are regular visitors. Divers have had success snorkeling with these beautiful animals, although keep an eye out for silky sharks, which often tag along.

TAMMY PELUSO

Orca whales are a delightful sight in late fall.

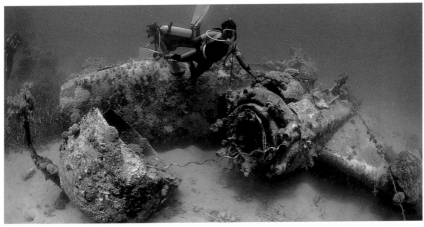

Divers escape blustery trade winds and get rare good visibility on the Hudson Aircraft.

Two dive sites on the northern side of Boia Boia Waga Island, where two reef points extend out from the island, have near vertical walls and depths of 8m on top. The sites are partly protected from the southeast tradewinds.

Mantas and hammerheads are sometimes seen in shallow water near the edge of the drop-off. Leaf and lacy scorpionfish are often found in the excellent coral growths. These dives are best when slight currents are flowing.

In Milne Bay, not far from East Cape, is the wreck of a **Hudson Aircraft** in 10m. The wreck is upside down and inaccessible for most of the year since southeast trade winds blow straight onto the site. During the northwest season the wreck is an interesting dive for aircraft enthusiasts, but otherwise has little to offer.

18 Banana Bommie

One of PNG's best dive sites is Banana Bommie, on which a ship ran aground a few years back. This caused a large scar on top of the reef that makes a convenient spot to anchor. The rest of the reef is brilliantly alive and, with a slight current from the west, it is a superb dive.

Around March/April millions of small baitfish gather on the reef, attracting pelagic predators such as Spanish mackerel and dogtooth tuna. The schools of baitfish scatter as the predators lunge through them.

Colorful soft corals, sea fans, sea whips and black corals adorn the sloping side of the reef, which drops to about

Location: 3km southeast of Boia Boia Waga Island

Depth Range: 4-30m (13-100ft)

Access: Boat

Expertise Rating: Intermediate

30m before leveling off in a sandy plain inhabited by huge garden eels and red-lined sea cucumbers. Batfish parade up and down the reef and several anemones with maroon spinecheeked anemonefish are easily found, with barramundi cod

BOB HALSTEAD

A rainbow of soft corals, sea fans and sea whips covers the
sloping side of Banana Bommie.

peering from their coral lairs. Many reef fish allow close approach and the red miniata cod are particularly obliging for underwater photographs.

Other similar sites in the area include **Greg's Reef**, a spur projecting from a larger reef, and **Telita Reef**, a double ridge bordering the deep outer drop-off.

19 North Coast

Along the north coast from East Cape are several very good dive sites that are close to shore and sheltered from strong trade winds, making the diving safe and easy. The narrow fringing reef along the shore drops precipitously to several hundred meters so the water is usually clear, and big animal encounters are common though not predictable.

Anchoring is not always easy since the fringing reef may be awash at low tide. **Wahoo Reef**, about 11km west of East Cape, is a convenient point where the drop-off makes a right angle turn into a bay. Boats should not anchor right on the point as beautiful stands of cabbage coral could easily be damaged; there is a suitable barren patch 50m to the east beside a small bommie.

Location: North coast, west of East Cape

Depth Range: 0-40m (0-130ft) plus

Access: Boat

Expertise Rating: Novice

Divers will get the best dive by swimming or slowly drifting along the edge of the drop-off in 15-20m, continuing around the point and into the bay, then returning in the shallows where there is no current. Avoid the temptation to dive too deep. The hammerhead sharks and other big animals common at this site will often swim over the heads of divers.

The rest of the reef is still recovering after damage by crown-of-thorns sea stars, although the shallow reef is pretty with interesting nooks and crannies to explore.

Dale's Reef, a few kilometers farther west, has spectacular coral gardens and the finest stand of cabbage coral to be found in PNG. Again take great care in anchoring and do not visit this site without local knowledge.

About 12km west of East Cape is **Basilisk Point**, a good dive site with excellent coral formations, which attract larger fish, sharks and rays. A wall falling from shallow water is rimmed with green tree coral. This changes to a sloping reef then abruptly back into another vertical drop with some dramatic crevices sliced into the wall.

BOB HALSTEAD

Shallow coral gardens at Dale's Reef.

20 Kathy's Corner

Kathy's Corner has a variety of different habitats without much big animal action, although turtles are common and a dugong lives in the area. The reef has a shallow labyrinth. When the sun is shining, it is a special site for wide-angle photographers. But the site also has excellent macro opportunities, with many species of nudibranchs making it a colorful night dive. The labyrinth has flashlightfish on dark nights, Spanish dancers are often found on the wall leading to it, and comet fish lurk deep in the crevices.

Adjacent to the wall off the beach is a dark sand slope with a couple of small patch reefs and a bonanza of fish life. Large lionfish hunt damsels and cardinalfish, and schools of striped snapper meander around the staghorn corals. A couple of small rocky outcrops from the

Location: Bay to east of Basilisk Point

Depth Range: 0-40m (0-130ft) plus

Access: Boat

Expertise Rating: Novice

reef are covered with stinging corallimorpharians and should not be touched.

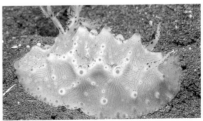
BOB HALSTEAD

Halgerda aurantiomaculata nudibranch.

Beware! Corallimorpharians: The Evil "Anemone"

These unassuming, disc-like critters resemble tiny sea anemones but are actually a close relative. They may be no larger than 10cm (4 inches) across and look olive-green or brown underwater. Getting too close to or touching Corallimorpharians can be dangerous because they have a powerful sting, sometimes made seaborne through a mass of white filaments the creature releases when disturbed. These can easily penetrate the skin, even through a Lycra suit.

Author Bob Halstead experienced these critters first-hand. He noticed a rash of small stings on his skin after one dive where many of these creatures clustered. The stings became more painful and eventually got to the point where his arm and shoulder were in great pain and became very weak. By the time he was diagnosed properly, his arm strength all but disappeared. It took six weeks for the pain to go away and a year of working with weights to get his strength back to normal.

Learn to look for these harmless-looking little critters and do not disturb them. The *Discosoma* genus is found throughout PNG. Look for it normally in small colonies, but it can form huge congregations in some areas.

21 Deacon's Reef & Dinah's Beach

Deacon's Reef and Dinah's Beach are two very special dive sites next to each other that are usually dived from a boat anchored off Lauadi village.

Deacon's Reef has a steep drop-off at the edge where a series of coral towers

Location: The bay west of Basilisk Point

Depth Range: 0-40m (0-130ft) plus

Access: Boat

Expertise Rating: Novice

An underwater view of a village canoe.

reaches to just a few meters from the surface. Between the towers and the cliff ashore is a gorgeous coral garden full of tropical fish, a giant sea fan and a forest of red sea whips. Several photographs of this reef were featured in the April 1988 issue of *National Geographic*—the view of the reef with the sun's rays streaming down through overhanging trees is one few divers will ever forget.

Hammerhead sharks and whale sharks are sometimes encountered along the reef edge. Although deep diving is tempting, divers are better advised to spend long dives in the shallows.

The dilemma at this site is whether to keep diving at Deacon's Reef or to spend more time at Dinah's Beach, which is famous for its splendid array of interesting and exotic marine creatures. Five species of lionfish, six species of anemonefish, blue ribbon eels, shrimp gobies, several families of octopus, cuttlefish, ghost pipefish, sea moths, mantis shrimp and giant corallimorpharians. The list is almost endless—all within 10m making marathon dives possible. The creatures here are used to divers and allow very close approach. Indeed, care needs to be taken since, particularly at dusk and at night, the lionfish have learned to follow divers around.

BOB HALSTEAD

An octopus is the center of attention at this Dinah's Beach cleaning station.

Emperor angelfish are common and can be observed in all colorful stages of growth, from blue and white juveniles to fantastically patterned adults. If you decide to reduce nitrogen loadings for a while there is a nice walk ashore, along a stream bed through rainforest to a stunning double waterfall.

22　Nuakata Island to Basilaki Island

Reefs and smaller islands inviting adventurers to some of the best diving in PNG surround Nuakata Island. Good things do not come easy however, and although the diving can be superb, strong currents and variable visibility can cause disappointment. Check out the Port Moresby tide tables for times of neap tides and gentle currents.

Visibility is largely unpredictable for much of the year. The island has several bays for secure anchorage and the village people enjoy coming out to trade shells and vegetables.

The west and south sides of the island harbor many small, isolated reefs, which rise from 60m or so, and make for won-

Location: Southeast of East Cape

Depth Range: 5-40m (16-130ft) plus

Access: Boat

Expertise Rating: Advanced

derful diving. Most of these can be circumnavigated on a single tank, but the best plan is to find the side of the reef receiving current. Here many schools of fish—redtooth triggerfish, midnight sea perch, rainbow runners and masses of

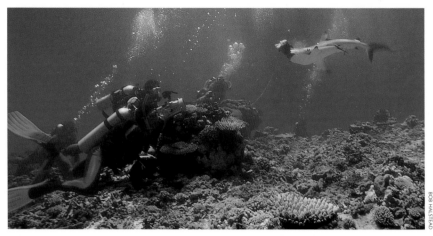

Divers look on as a grey reef shark takes a bait by Jeremy's Reef.

fusiliers and surgeonfish—parade along the edge of the reef. Spanish mackerel, dogtooth tuna and grey reef sharks hunt in the abundance. Manta rays, and their smaller relatives the mobula, are also regularly seen.

Most of the action takes place in relatively shallow water just over the edge of the reef (some of the reefs do not have enough water on top to permit safe passage even in small boats) and most divers choose to dive to modest depths, spending more time in the shallows. Giant clams are common on top among the staghorn and plate corals, orange sea fans and anemones.

Some of the favorite reefs include **Black & Silver Reef**, which features a forest of two species of black coral. The deeper variety, starting at 22m, has ghostly silver polyps. **Nuakata Bay Reef** is the smaller of a pair of reefs connected by a deep ridge and has excellent fish life and a healthy mixture hard and soft corals. **Tunnel Reef** has a beautiful swim-through starting at 27m and rising to 15m at its southern end, with a triple stand of vertical coral towers at the other.

Mike's Reef is an exquisite coral bommie loaded with so much life. It is connected to a larger reef—suitable for anchoring—by a ridge featuring a magnificent display of sea fans. **Bob's Bommie** has a single coral tower standing on its western end, necessitating a swim across the deep channel. Black coral trees decorate the side of the tower, and a colorful swim-through pierces the top.

Heinecke Heaven is uncharted with 13m of water to its top. This reef has exceptionally colorful soft corals and a good population of grey reef sharks. Being somewhat isolated from the other reefs, it acts like an oasis for marine life.

The dramatic swim-through at Bob's Bommie.

23 Peer's Reef

On the northern side of Nuakata Island, the outer reefs boarder a deep drop-off and provide opportunities for hammerhead shark encounters. Schools of up to 50 hammerheads are sometimes seen in the southeast season, along with many other large pelagics.

Location: Northeast of Nuakata Island

Depth Range: 5-40m (16-130ft) plus

Access: Boat

Expertise Rating: Advanced

The reef is named after Peer Kirkemo, who loved diving here and who was tragically killed in a car accident in Port Moresby. A memorial to him has been placed on the reef at 31m at the spot where he used to sit to watch the action. This can be a very difficult dive with a current often reaching one to two knots. Divers should set up a drift dive, dropping in up-current along the reef and then drifting back to the anchored boat.

24 Boirama Reef

Boirama Reef, in the passage between Nuakata Island and Boirama Island, has a small drop-off on its southern side near the white sandy beach off Boirama Island. Soft corals, sponges and sea fans are abundant and smothered with a multitude of crinoids. Barracuda, batfish, surgeonfish, sweetlips and clouds of smaller fish hang out along the front face. The top of the reef, which features some magnificent giant clams, has coral heads and sand gutters at 8m.

Location: East of Nuakata Island

Depth Range: 0-40m (0-130ft) plus

Access: Boat

Expertise Rating: Advanced

If the current is too fierce for comfort, divers can be dropped up-current to make an easy drift dive back to the boat. Alternatively, the reef on the south side of the sandy beach may be dived. This reef is less affected by the current and has some beautiful delicate coral growths and more than its fair share of butterflyfish.

A giant clam thrives in the shallow, protected garden.

25 | Gallows Reef

Gallows Reef is a large horseshoe reef open on its western side, with many patch reefs and passes on its northern and southern sides.

Location: East of Nuakata Island

Depth Range: 5-40m (16-130ft) plus

Access: Boat

Expertise Rating: Intermediate

Anemone Reef has a fine example of a colonial anemone inhabited by hundreds of red and black anemonefish. A giant clam sits at the edge of the colonial and is popular with photographers.

The **North Pass** has several dive sites, the bommies on the western side having the best coral growth. Sand tilefish and wrasses—including one undescribed species of sand-diving wrasse—populate the deeper sand slopes.

Anemone crab

Spinecheek anemonefish

Anemone Homes & Residents

Ten different species of anemonefish are found in PNG. One to look for is the white-bonnet anemonefish. Lone individuals of this species tend to share a host anemone with another different species of anemonefish. The clown or percula anemonefish is probably the most photographed and most colorful of them all. The anemones vary greatly and host a variety of shrimps including the red-capped shrimp, magnificent shrimp and the short-capped shrimp. Look for the porcelain crab in the short-tentacled anemones.

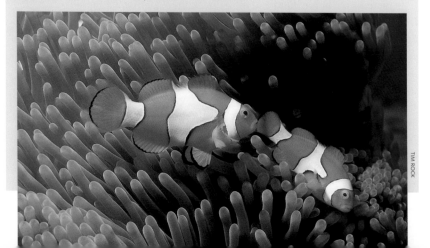

26 Doubilet Reef & Basilaki Island

Doubilet Reef is one of the finest reefs in Milne Bay but not always accessible, mainly because of currents. It has an incredible forest of pink sea fans on its slopes with red sea whips, black corals and barrel sponges scattered among them. The top has a beautiful coral garden with big plate corals in shallow water.

Take care to anchor only in the few rubble areas. A nearby deep channel attracts large marine animals including giant groupers and silvertip sharks.

Visibility in the area is highly variable. It's best to explore the passes in the ribbon reef near the islands, and the patch reefs on the sides receiving current.

In calm weather **Waterman Ridge** and **Denlay Reef** can be dived on the southeast side of Grant Island. These are stacked with fish, hard and soft corals and gorgonians on an interesting series of reef fingers and isolated bommies. In windy southeast conditions, the northern side of Grant Island is sheltered and has good marine life, particularly to the east.

Location: Between Basilaki & Blakeney Island

Depth Range: 8-40m (26-130ft) plus

Access: Boat

Expertise Rating: Advanced

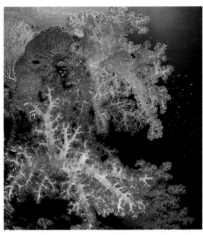

Soft corals and sea fans thrive in the current.

27 P38 Lightning Aircraft Wreck

Inside the excellent sheltered anchorage of Basilaki Bay—the western of two large bays on the northern side of Basilaki Island—lies the wreck of a mag-

Location: Basilaki Bay

Depth: 27m (90ft)

Access: Boat

Expertise Rating: Intermediate

nificent P38 Lightning Aircraft near the western entrance. This famous single-seater fighter was ditched (probably in 1943), and while the pilot survived, any records of the flight have apparently been lost. The aircraft's radio call sign is 2-66869.

The aircraft was found intact except for its propellers. In 1995 the propellers were located and recovered where the aircraft hit the water. They now rest next to their respective engines on the wreck. It is important to note that all war relics are protected in PNG and nothing should be removed from any wrecks.

There are several anemones and their fish on the wreck and regularly seen fish include crocodilefish, sweetlips and the occasional wobbegong shark. The wreck lies in 27m with its guns pointing at a reef that rises to convenient anchoring depths. Although silty and sometimes murky, the reef has good marine life and boasts critters not found elsewhere, such as the rare jawfish and even rarer "hairy" ghost pipefish.

28 China Strait & Samarai

The first European to enter Milne Bay was Captain John Moresby in 1873, when he sailed into China Strait, which he named thinking he had discovered a shortcut from Australia to China. The Strait is 2km or so wide, 35 to 50m deep, and has fierce currents running through it. This was one of the most popular places for pre-war, hard-hat pearl divers, who harvested the gold lip pearl shells.

Experienced sport divers can get a thrill by trying a drift dive through the strait at 4-5 knots, hanging from a weighted line trailing from a drifting boat. The effect is like underwater water skiing.

Tiny Samarai Island has a spectacular wharf dive. The island is a romantic reminder of PNG's colonial history, and welcomes visitors with a natural warmth

Location: Southern entrance to Milne Bay

Depth Range: 5-40m (16-130ft) plus

Access: Boat

Expertise Rating: Advanced

typical of Milne Bay. The views are superb and the surrounding islands offer good snorkeling but only modest diving.

A P40 Kittyhawk aircraft wreck rests in 12m between two islands, at the northern entrance to China Strait. It can be dived at slack tide. The tail is missing and the wreck is badly corroded but it is still worth a look.

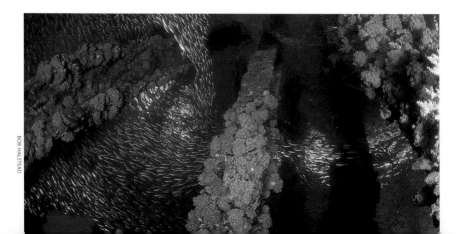

BOB HALSTEAD

29 | Daisy's Drop-Off

A high and steep-sided rock found west of Wari Island has a ledge on its northern side suitable for anchoring. Underwater the wall drops to about 40m. The prevailing and sometimes very strong current moves along the face of the wall and over the ledge. Divers should be dropped in the water up-current, then make a controlled drift dive to the ledge.

Location: West of Wari Island

Depth Range: 5-40m (16-130ft) plus

Access: Boat

Expertise Rating: Advanced

The soft coral growth on the wall is incredible, and fish life is abundant. This is one of the richest soft coral gardens in the whole of PNG, but requires considerable skill to handle the currents that have caused the amazing fertility of the reef.

Fantastic fish, fans and corals at Daisy's Drop-Off.

30 | *President Grant*

The *President Grant* ran aground on Uluma Reef shortly after WWII and has broken up in the swells that crash during

Location: Uluma Reef south of Wari Island

Depth Range: 0-10m (0-33ft)

Access: Boat

Expertise Rating: Intermediate

the southeast trade wind season. Even during calm weather swells can be a problem. However, if the sea is flat, this can be a fascinating dive.

A large deck gun sits upright on the bottom, surrounded by wreckage including large boilers, machinery and scattered machine guns. The wreck has large populations of resident fish and the water is usually very clear.

31 Sawa Sawaga

This is an extraordinary current dive, although not for the faint-hearted. The safest plan is to drift through the eastern side of the passage at 10m, when the current is running from the south. A deeper

Location: Between Sidea & Sariba Islands

Depth Range: 0-30m (0-100ft)

Access: Boat

Expertise Rating: Advanced

TIM ROCK

Yellow and black crinoids cling to a fan.

drift can take you into violent, out-of-control depth changes.

The views are truly spectacular with huge numbers fish along ledges and boulders covered in multi-hued soft corals. The perfect end to the dive is an ascent up the slope to beautiful coral gardens shallower than one meter right next to the shore.

32 Giants at Home

After many years of searching, a principal cleaning station for giant manta rays was recently discovered. Here the mantas are present throughout the day and take turns approaching a small, isolated bommie where they get cleaned by small wrasses. While hovering over the bommie, the mantas will allow divers close approach.

The cleaning station is dominated by some of the largest mantas ever seen in Milne Bay, with wingspans stretching 4 to 5m. A significant proportion of the mantas are "Darth Vadar" black all over,

Location: Near China Strait

Depth Range: 5-15m (16-49ft)

Access: Boat

Expertise Rating: Intermediate

which is common in the Indo-Pacific. It is also possible to snorkel with feeding mantas. This beautiful sheltered dive site is destined to become one of PNG's most famous.

D'Entrecasteaux Islands & Tufi Dive Sites

The D'Entrecasteaux Islands and Tufi have some of PNG's most dramatic landscapes. The D'Entrecasteaux group contains areas of old volcanic cones and active hot springs. It includes Goodenough Island which, although only 40km (24 miles) long, rises to 2,566m (8419ft). This island is incredibly beautiful with steep, almost vertical sides and twin peaks.

Deep in the interior, amateur (and professional) anthropologists will want to see the black-and-white stone, a rock covered in black and white paintings that are said to predict the success of the yam crops.

To the north of the D'Entrecasteaux lie the infamous Trobriand Islands—the Islands of Love. This sobriquet always raises interest but there are some pretty complicated social norms within the Trobriands that might surprise any outsider hoping for an island fling. Still, the freedom of the society and the easy-going people make this an interesting stopover.

The land geography of Tufi is also worth a look. Tufi is famous for its deep fjords that slice through the hills, eventually rising to the peak of Mount Victory at 1,883m (6178ft). The fjord and Tufi wharf are pictured here.

Weather Conditions

WIND: The southeast trade winds blow from May through November, but are often countered by land breezes from the mountains behind Tufi. From January until April light winds blow from the northwest. Strong northwesterlies tend to be short, lasting only few hours.

RAIN: The driest months of the year are June through October, corresponding to the steady southeast trade winds. Rainfall the rest of the year does not vary significantly.

WATER TEMPERATURE: The average lows are around 26°C (79°F) in June/July and highs around 29°C (84°F) in January/February.

BOB HALSTEAD

The gun on the *S'Jacob* is obscured by fish and heavy marine growth.

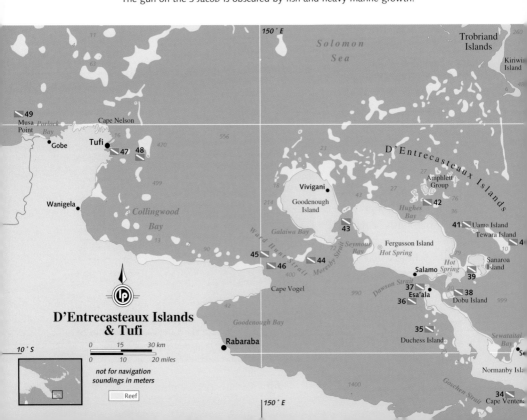

D'Entrecasteaux & Tufi Diving

The drama of Tufi continues on the scattered offshore reefs. Most of these are uncharted and many are yet to be dived. This is one of the more popular places for the live-aboards to do discovery dives to find new sites. The variety seems endless and stumbling on a manta cleaning station or a new hammerhead site is always a possibility.

Like most of the islands in the area, the reefs are an eye-catching combination of hard and soft corals. In the narrow straits, whales, dolphins and dugongs are common. Schooling fish are also prolific.

There are also many good muck diving sites here, requiring astute powers of observation and patience, but with very rewarding results.

D'Entrecasteaux Islands & Tufi Dive Sites	Good Snorkeling	Novice	Intermediate	Advanced
33 Cape Ventenat	●		●	
34 Bunama		●		
35 West Coast of Normanby Island	●		●	
36 Balaban's Bommie	●	●		
37 Observation Point	●	●		
38 Bubble Bath	●	●		
39 Sanaroa Passage	●		●	
40 Sanaroa's Offshore Reefs	●			●
41 Wong's Reef				●
42 North Side of Fergusson Island	●		●	
43 Moresby Strait	●		●	
44 Dart Reefs	●			●
45 Keast Reef				●
46 B17 Bomber "Blackjack"				●
47 Tufi Wharf	●		●	
48 Tufi Offshore Reefs	●		●	
49 S'Jacob				●

33 Cape Ventenat

Cape Ventenat has two islands and a barrier reef off its south side. Although mostly uncharted, the barrier reef continues along the eastern side of Normanby Island. In the northwest trade wind season the reef is sheltered and can be dived at several places.

Linda's Reef is a particularly lively site at the northern end of one of the sausage-shaped patches that make up the barrier.

The best diving conditions are when a slight current is flowing on to the sloping face of the reef, which drops to a sandy bottom at about 50m. The reef has good sea fans and soft corals at 30m. The fish life is prolific and there are usually sever-

Location: Southeast tip of Normanby Island

Depth Range: 5-40m (16-130ft) plus

Access: Boat

Expertise Rating: Intermediate

al grey reef sharks swimming about. The tops of these reefs receive a pounding in the southeast season and are therefore not as attractive as some of the more sheltered reefs. If the current is flowing, setting up a drift dive along the wall on the northern side of the islands is recommended.

34 Bunama

Bunama is a mission station with bays on both sides. The bottom is silty with algae and sea grass beds in the shallows and, although it looks unappealing at first, the area is full of surprises. The western bay is most popular and has a

Location: South coast of Normanby Island

Depth Range: 0-30m (0-100ft)

Access: Boat

Expertise Rating: Novice

BOB HALSTEAD
Panda clownfish adults and juveniles.

huge, shallow population of sand anemones inhabited by panda clownfish. This is one of the few places that the large black-and-white adults are found together with the juveniles and sub-adults, which have yellow patches.

The anemones also are home to porcelain crabs. Other fascinating creatures found in the algae and grass beds include seahorses, ghost pipefish, double-ended pipefish, frogfish, cowfish, octopus, squid and cuttlefish. The site makes a good night dive since many different species of shells, including the fabulous Venus comb murex, can be found with careful searching. Remember that collecting live shells in PNG is strictly forbidden.

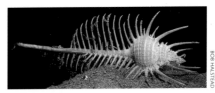

Murex shells scavenge and prey upon bivalves.

35 West Coast of Normanby Island

Duchess Island is in the middle of an extensive but inaccurately charted reef system. Some of these reefs lie up to 8 km offshore and are awash at low tide, presenting a significant hazard to careless navigators. But the diving on these reefs is excellent.

Location: West Coast of Normanby

Depth Range: 0-40m (0-130ft) plus

Access: Boat

Expertise Rating: Intermediate

Calypso Reef was first dived in 1988 when Cousteau's *Calypso* used it when filming in PNG. The reef has an extensive sunken ribbon extending on its northern end with depths of 6m and deeper. Take care anchoring and select one of the few barren patches to prevent damaging the beautiful coral growths.

Giant barrel sponges are common and the reef is covered with a colorful carpet of crinoids. This is a good site to find the elusive lacy scorpionfish. There are two vertical drop-offs, the western one descending to over 300m and the eastern to a lagoon floor at about 60m. However, most of the action takes place in the shallows.

Nearby is **Chris's Reef**, featuring a large and perfect stand of cabbage coral. Good night anchorage can be obtained at "J Bay" in nearby Normanby Island. Vessels using the bay are advised to slow down before entering to prevent wash damage to the villagers' fishing nets.

Corals, sea fans and whips flourish in the D'Entrecasteaux Islands.

If the wind is blowing, you can find shelter behind Duchess Island, which has interesting shallow diving off the sand spit on its eastern side. Anchor cautiously as strong gusts of wind can suddenly strike the boat, pushing it toward the reef or causing the anchor to drag.

Sailing northwest from Duchess Island (with caution!) you'll find other spectacular reefs. **Pohle Reef** has a beautiful undercut drop-off on its western side. At its northwest extremity a short ridge enables boats to safely anchor. The rest of the reef is too shallow.

36 Balaban's Bommie

Balaban's Bommie has vertical drop-offs on its southern side and southwestern tip (the only place suitable for anchoring). There is a steep coral slope with caves and swim-throughs on the northwestern side and a coral crest and sand slope around the rest.

On top of the reef, which is less than 2m deep, on the northern side, is one of the most exquisite hard coral reefs found in all of PNG.

Although damaged by coral bleaching in 1996, the reef is recovering well. A variety of old growth corals in perfect condition compete with each other for

Location: Off northwest tip of Normanby Island

Depth Range: 0-40m (0-130ft) plus

Access: Boat

Expertise Rating: Novice

space. This is a superb snorkeling site and the conditions are often calm, as the land breezes from the mountains of nearby Fergusson Island counter the trade winds.

37 Observation Point

Observation Point is perfectly protected from the southeast trade winds by Normanby Island. Village boats have traditionally used the site as a resting place before the long haul to East Cape.

The bottom is sandy with outcrops of algae and sea grass. Part of it is a constantly changing loose sand slope, descending from the surface to 35m. Debris of leaves and twigs accumulates in a hollow in the sand. Reef and mangroves extend along the northern side.

Striped shrimpfish and silver moonfish swarm in the shallows. Ghost pipefish hide among the sand crinoids. Flying gurnards skim along the sand as

Location: Northwest tip of Normanby Island

Depth Range: 0-35m (0-115ft)

Access: Boat

Expertise Rating: Novice

peacock flounders hunt the several species of sand divers. Razorfish dive into the sand and shrimp gobies stand guard while the shrimps bulldoze their homes clean. Rare striped octopus and flamboyant cuttlefish have been photographed here. Demon stingers, and many of their scorpionfish relatives, shuffle across the sand.

For lovers of the bizarre this dive is like a treasure hunt—it is a sophisticated dive (requiring skill in observation)—and can be incredibly rewarding.

A flounder rests stealthily in the sand.

Shallows at Observation Point.

38 | Bubble Bath

As you sail east through Dawson Strait between Normanby and Fergusson Islands, a vision of tropical splendor greets the eye. Old volcanic cones are evident among the rainforest slopes of the mountains. Steam rises from thermal springs. Canoes and small boats make their way across the calm waters.

Dobu Island at the eastern end of the Dawson Strait has a "Bubble Bath" in shallow water near its northeastern point. One giant vent continually gushes volcanic gas bubbles from the bottom. Surprisingly, the area is alive with all the usual shallow reef inhabitants and the bubbles make for interesting and unique photographs.

The villagers here are keen to trade sea shells and vegetables from their fertile gardens. A visit to Dobu is always a pleasure.

Location: Dobu Island

Depth Range: 0-10m (0-33ft)

Access: Boat

Expertise Rating: Novice

Hot volcanic bubbles gush from the bottom vents.

39 Sanaroa Passage

In the sheltered waters between Fergusson and Sanaroa Islands is a beautiful area of lush reefs. Tidal currents push the deep water back and forth through the passage, providing nutrients for the soft corals and sea fans that thrive on the reefs.

Location: Between Sanaroa and Fergusson Islands

Depth Range: 5-40m (16-130ft)

Access: Boat

Expertise Rating: Intermediate

Double Tower is one of the most impressive sites, consisting of a pair of coral towers joined to a larger reef by a saddle. The top of the eastern tower is quite barren and suitable for anchoring at 8m. Its sides are covered with colorful sea fans, whips and sponges. The second tower has magnificent growths all over it. Between the towers at 30m is a small drop-off to 40m, where a forest of grey sea whips decorates the edge.

At **Sonia Shoal** to the west, when a strong current flows from the north, back eddies make it possible to circumnavigate virtually the whole reef counter-clockwise. Boats must only anchor in sand patches on the western side of the reef as much of the eastern side is covered with a magnificent stand of cabbage coral.

Nearby **Rhino Reef** is named for the regular sightings of the lacy scorpionfish. Two dives are possible on this reef, depending on the direction of the current. It is always best to dive the side receiving current since that is where the fish will hang out. Both sites have a sloping drop-off to 40m with excellent sea fans and soft coral growth. The shallow reeftop has sand gutters and rich reef patches featuring green tree coral.

Valley Reef is farther north and closer to Sanaroa Island. It has a small bommie suitable for anchoring, connected by a saddle to a long narrow reef with several side branches. A valley between this and another patch reef closer to Sanaroa has some large sea fans. Visibility is rarely less than 40m, except in the northwest season after heavy rain. It is possible to dive the eastern side of Sanaroa Island, which is typically clear all year but inaccessible in the southeast trade winds.

BOB HALSTEAD

Double Tower has many lush colorful sea fans.

Scoping Scorpionfish

On top of PNG's coral-laden reefs you will find a huge variety of reef fish, a marine population so abundant and unique, that you'll never stop talking about all the fish you saw. Of particular interest—both for its beauty and rarity—is the lacy scorpionfish, which sits in the open looking much like a feather star. The leaf scorpionfish, which likes to perch on staghorn coral branches, occurs in white, yellow, violet or black.

Lacy Scorpionfish

40 Sanaroa's Offshore Reefs

In calm weather boats cruising near Sanaroa can head out into the Solomon Sea, where a series of unsurveyed reefs radiate southeast from Uama and Tewara Islands.

End Pass is the end of a ribbon reef. Sharks are common in the area and divers use the remote reef as a feeding station. Pelagics patrol the edge of the reef, which has healthy growths of hard corals.

Hickson's Reef is actually two reefs separated by a channel. There are large sea fans on the western side. Several dives are possible; however, the best fish action is at the southeast corner where the consistent but slight current meets the reef. Dogtooth tuna, Spanish mackerel and whitetip reef sharks mingle with clouds of fusiliers and surgeonfish. The reeftop at 8m has extensive growths of staghorn coral. There are soft corals and whips deeper down the drop-off.

Mary Jane (MJ) Reef and **Suzy's Reef** are closer to Tewara Island—only about 6km to the east. Both have large sea fans, black corals and whips. These are beautifully positioned so that photographers can shoot upwards into the sun. There

Location: Northwest of Sanaroa Island

Depth Range: 5-40m (16-130ft) plus

Access: Boat

Expertise Rating: Advanced

are many other possible dive sites in this largely unexplored area.

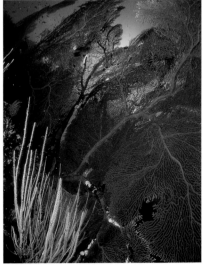

Red fans and whips make great photo subjects.

41 Wong's Reef

Wong's Reef near Uama island has a sheer drop-off on its south face. A deep descending ridge decorated with huge black coral trees falls at 25m and deeper. This is where the fish usually hang out with the typical southeast ocean current. The reef is partly sheltered but the current can be fierce at times. A gutter on the western side separates Wong's Reef from an adjacent reef, behind which are brilliant stands of sea fans and soft corals.

Below that is a sandy plateau beyond 30m, full of garden eels and other sand-dwelling critters. The reef, surrounded by many giant clams and a rich coral garden, has a barren mound on top in 5m

Location: West of Uama Island

Depth Range: 0-40m (0-130ft) plus

Access: Boat

Expertise Rating: Advanced

suitable for anchoring. Striped sweetlips school at the front of the reef and a large school of bumphead parrotfish graze on the corals. The reef has spectacular numbers and varieties of anthias, butterflyfish and angelfish, with visibility reliably in excess of 40m.

BOB HALSTEAD

42 North Side of Fergusson Island

Several uncharted reefs lie between Fergusson Island and the Amphlett Islands, which is a group of small, sheer-sided small islands whose villagers are renowned for their finely crafted clay pots.

Humann's Colour Book is a narrow patch reef about 5km south of Yabwaia Island. The eastern side of the reef catches the prevailing current. The result is a kaleidoscopically colorful dive, decorated with soft corals, gorgonians and schools of parading reef fish.

The narrow reef is not easy to anchor on. The surface can become choppy in the southeast trade wind season, when the land breezes from Fergusson Island die down. Farther south is **Humann's Shark Reef**, which has a healthy and lively population of grey reef sharks.

In the pass between Wawiwa and Yabwaia Islands, **Amphlett Fans** is a

Location: North Side of Fergusson

Depth Range: 5-40m (16-130ft)

Access: Boat

Expertise Rating: Intermediate

small patch reef surrounded by huge sea fans, unusual sponges and hard corals. Eagle rays sometimes feed in the sand gutters around the reef. Anchoring is not advised close to the reef. Damage could easily occur, particularly when the southeast winds produce a funneling effect causing sudden and severe gusts. This is not a good anchorage in anything but calm conditions.

Several good dives notable for luxuriant sponge gardens are found elsewhere

BOB HALSTEAD

Steady currents create just the right conditions for stunning marine growth at Humann's Colour Book.

in the Amphlett Group, particularly off the west side of Wamea Island.

At the northwestern tip of Fergusson Island are some convenient reefs close to shore. **Trotman Shoals**, a series of four small patch reefs, are only 3km off Cape Labillardiere and are small enough to easily circumnavigate on a single dive. A kilometer to the north is a more complex reef system known as **Knight Patches**, which feature some particularly photogenic coral formations. Sharks are occasionally seen here. The water in the area is invariably clear—visibility is rarely below 40m—and the region is sheltered from the southeast trade winds.

43 Moresby Strait

In Moresby Strait, between Fergusson and Goodenough Islands, there is interesting diving at **Mapamoiwa Reef**, a small patch reef 6km north of the mission station at Mapamoiwa. This reef has a sheer vertical drop-off on its western side and a seascape of small towers, valleys and mini drop-offs on its eastern side. Many other reefs in the area have good fish life but visibility is variable and sometimes reduced to 15m. Some of the reefs are very shallow.

Good overnight anchorage can be found at Mapamoiwa Anchorage, where the small wharf should be kept clear for village use. It is convenient to anchor a few meters to the north of the wharf on a steep sand slope adjacent to a reef. Tie the stern to a tree branch overhanging the

Location: Between Fergusson and Goodenough Islands

Depth Range: 0-40m (0-130ft) plus

Access: Boat

Expertise Rating: Intermediate

beach. The shallows have sea grass beds with a selection of fascinating critters, especially interesting at night. Panda clownfish are common as are dwarf lionfish, shrimpfish and shrimp gobies. Yellow frogfish and seahorses have also been seen. The views here are spectacular.

TIM ROCK

A hermit crab finds a new home.

BOB HALSTEAD

Look carefully for the eye of the yellow frogfish.

44 Dart Reefs

Goodenough Island is an imposing presence. High enough to produce its own weather, it has some outstanding diving off its south coast. Several good overnight anchorages include Galaiwa Bay, where you'll find some of the friendliest people anywhere. There is a large lagoon inland of the anchorage that is well worth exploring in a dinghy.

Wagifa anchorage is good in the northwest season and you'll likely be surrounded by dozens of young people, laughing and chattering, with shells and vegetables for sale.

Between Goodenough Island and Cape Vogel on the mainland is the wonderland of uncharted reefs known as Dart Reefs.

A couple of kilometers off the entrance to Galaiwa Bay is **Cecilia's Reef**, a tiny patch reef that should only be dived in calm conditions. The reeftop at 5m has delicate stands of staghorn coral, and the rubble patch used for anchorage is rather small.

The reef attracts many species of fish and is small enough to be easily circumnavigated. Lacy scorpionfish are

Location: Between Goodenough Island & Cape Vogel

Depth Range: 2-40m (7-130ft) plus

Access: Boat

Expertise Rating: Advanced

Bright red bigeye drift in small schools.

commonly found and the vertical reef walls are adorned with small fans and sea whips. Dusk and night dives are particularly worthwhile.

Camel Reef to the southeast is an ascending ridge culminating in a double hump and separated by a saddle. Boats should anchor in the rubble patch west of the two humps in 8m.

The first hump has an unusual stand of pillar coral, decorated with crinoids, but the second hump is the best. A slight current from the east provides perfect conditions and schools of larger fish mill around the hump.

About 8km northwest of Galaiwa Bay is a series of reefs known as **Peer's Patches**. The small western-most bommie is used for anchoring. A canyon to the east, separates it from two larger patch reefs. The channel walls have abundant growths of green tree coral

Galaiwa Bay and Goodenough Island.

and sea whips. Diving to the white sand floor of the canyon at maximum depth is worthwhile, as sharks often swim above.

At **See & Sea Passes**, a long ribbon reef is sliced in three places, forming two patch reefs and three passes. The passes allow water movement through the reef system, attracting large numbers of fish. The two patch reefs have about 8m of water on top and either of them can be anchored on, but take care to use the avaliable sandy patches. The western sides of the reefs are vertical, while the eastern slope is more gradual. Sharks are common.

45 Keast Reef

For some amazing fish action cruise to this isolated reef shown on the chart as Keast Reef. The reef is exposed but often accessible. Conditions are best with a slight current from the southeast.

The reeftop is under 5m though there are a couple of shallower patches. The best approach is from the southeast, anchoring as close to the vertical, deep drop-off as possible. Plenty of

Location: West of Dart Reefs

Depth Range: 5-40m (16-130ft) plus

Access: Boat

Expertise Rating: Advanced

Trevally cruise in thick schools at Keast Reef.

bare patches on the reeftop were badly damaged by crown-of-thorns sea stars a few years back. The reef is now recovering fast.

Descending the drop-off, divers are greeted by masses of fish including great schools of dogtooth tuna, bigeye trevally, surgeonfish, pinjalo, ocean triggerfish, barracuda and fusiliers. Sharks are often seen, including silvertips. This is one of the best dives in Milne Bay Province for pelagic fish action.

46 B17 Bomber "Blackjack"

Arguably the best aircraft wreck dive in the world rests at Cape Vogel. Rodney Pearce, who now operates the *Barbarian 2* live-aboard out of Lae, found the B17 Bomber "Blackjack" in 1986, in virtually perfect condition at 48m.

Villagers at Boga Boga village on the northern tip of the Cape tell the incredible story of how the Blackjack was

Location: Cape Vogel, off Boga Boga village

Depth: 48m (158ft)

Access: Boat

Expertise Rating: Advanced

The B17 Bomber "Blackjack"

Recent soft coral growth on the tailfin of the B17, which rests in very deep water.

ditched early one morning during WWII, right in front of their village. The villagers tell how they rescued all the crew members from the wrecked aircraft.

There is a very shallow reef in front of Boga Boga and then a steep wall to deep water. The dive is not an easy one since, in addition to being deep and exposed, there is often a current. The water is usually clear, but calm weather is necessary to dive this site.

The inside of the wreck, including the cockpit, can be seen and photographed through the various openings. Do not enter as there are many loose hanging wires. Blackjack had an amazing war history, which has been traced and the story made into a film, *Blackjack's Last Mission.*

47   Tufi Wharf

At Cape Nelson, along the north coast from Milne Bay, deep fjords cut into the mountain slopes. Perched on the tip of a hilly tentacle of land dividing two fjords is Tufi, a small town whose claim to fame was as a PT boat base during WWII. The scattered remains of two PT boats, including a deck gun and loaded torpedo tube, can still be seen at 40m directly down from the Tufi Wharf.

After diving the remains of the wrecks, ascend and swim to the left of the wharf where a scruffy coral garden

Location: Tufi

Depth Range: 0-40m (0-130ft)

Access: Boat or shore

Expertise Rating: Intermediate

hides many fascinating creatures including a multitude of nudibranchs.

48 Tufi Offshore Reefs

Offshore, dozens of reefs rise from 60m or more to the surface. This is an untouched coral wonderland with exciting and completely wild marine life.

Location: East of Tufi Harbour

Depth Range: 5-40m (16-130ft) plus

Access: Boat

Expertise Rating: Intermediate

Although the reefs are exposed, the sea is often calmer than you might expect, as land breezes from Mount Victory and Mount Trafalgar behind Tufi counter the trade winds.

Stewart Reef is one of the easier reefs to locate being a only a few minutes' boat ride east of the Tufi Wharf. It is marked by a red navigation light. The reef has a wall on its east side and a slope on its west. The wall is more interesting and has good growths of soft corals, fans and a very healthy fish population. The light makes the reef ideal for night diving.

Tony's Bommie features regular manta ray and giant grouper sightings and has a saddle at 40m where divers can look up at schools of barracuda, sharks and pelagics. This lively reef is about 15km southeast of Tufi.

A small sand caye, a seabird rookery, marks **Cyclone Reef**. Snorkelers and beginning divers will enjoy the shallow reef near the caye—look for the six giant clams—while more experienced divers

will find exciting diving over the wall on the edge of the reef.

A little farther from Tufi, 22km southeast, the water drops off the continental shelf to 600m or more. Reefs perched on the edge of this abyss are particularly exciting and likely to produce sightings of larger pelagics, such as hammerhead sharks.

Veale Reef is also conveniently signposted with a navigational beacon and is shown on the chart. This is an excellent dive, particularly if a slight current is flowing from the southeast. There are several dives here but the easterly wall has the steep drop. The ends of the reef are also interesting with deep crevices and overhangs. The water is usually very clear.

49 S'Jacob

The big attraction is to the northwest of Tufi is the incredible WWII wreck of the *S'Jacob*. Over 10km from land, the wreck is difficult to pinpoint without GPS navigation. It is 100m long, upright and sitting in 55m. The wreck supports huge resident populations of marine life. It has never been salvaged and is without doubt one of the world's greatest wreck dives.

Being exposed, the wreck is not always possible to dive, though land breezes do offer some protection in the mornings. Take care as the sea can become quite choppy very quickly when the land breezes subside.

The shallowest part of the wreck is the top of the enormous funnel at 35m. It is possible to make an exciting dive without going deeper than 40m, but the bridge and guns on the bow and stern are at 50m depths. A paravane used to snag mines rests on the starboard deck among many other artifacts not commonly seen on wrecks due to souveniring. This wreck is protected and salvaging is strictly forbidden.

Large stingrays and manta rays are commonly seen, as are giant groupers. The wreck is covered with black corals and has a permanent sheen of glittering bait fish. Redbar anthias, uncommon elsewhere, are abundant here. Tiger sharks appear on occasion. The bottom visibility is usually clearer than the surface layers. Much depends on tide and rainfall ashore, but 30m visibility is possible more often than not.

Location: North of Cape Nelson

Depth Range: 35-55m (115-180ft)

Access: Live-aboard

Expertise Rating: Advanced

A diver explores the *S'Jacob's* forward deck ladder.

BOB HALSTEAD

Lae Dive Sites

Lae is one of PNG's more developed areas with businesses, a university, an ecology institute and botanical gardens, a bustling harbor, a golf course and plenty of places to eat and stay. As the gateway to the Highlands of PNG, Lae is serviced several times a day by Air Niugini flights from Port Moresby but the drive from the airport at Nadzab—45km (28 miles) away—takes longer than the flight from Moresby.

The tiny, often insecure marina is choked with trading vessels and private boats. Visitors may wonder if they are in their right minds coming to such a place! However, there are a few oases of relaxed tropical charm in Lae, even though most tourists use the town as a stepping stone to more pleasant surroundings.

Lae has been described as a scruffy sort of place, but it does have its charm. It is large enough, unfortunately, to encompass some of the poorer qualities of PNG cities. There are no taxis, so after dark you are pretty much stuck at the hotel if you don't have a rental car. It is unsafe to walk anywhere in the evenings, and you are not allowed to anyway. Find a nice hotel or one with a shuttle service to the local restaurants.

The hovering mountains of the Highlands surround Lae and people seem to pay more attention to this aspect of life than to the seaward activities. It has become a major port, as coffee and tea are brought down from the Highlands. The town is major land hub as well, with lands spurring to the important towns in the mountains.

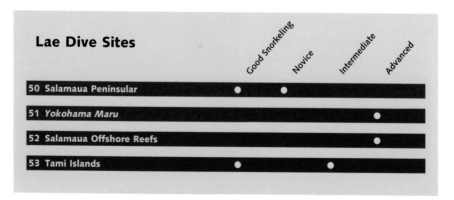

Lae Dive Sites	Good Snorkeling	Novice	Intermediate	Advanced
50 Salamaua Peninsular	●	●		
51 *Yokohama Maru*			●	
52 Salamaua Offshore Reefs			●	
53 Tami Islands	●		●	

Lae Diving

Lae is at the mouth of the Markham River, which constantly spews a plume of mud, staining the ocean surface. Fortunately, the sea is extremely deep right up to the coast, and the dirty water soon disperses.

BOB HALSTEAD

Giant whale sharks feed at Lae's deep drop-offs.

Fish life is good all around the area and odd creatures like the lacy scorpionfish are a real find for fish photographers and amateur ichthyologists. Whale sharks are known to feed at some sites.

One of the nicest dive areas is the Salamaua Peninsula, about 40km (25 miles) south of Lae. Here, beautiful shallow coral gardens and deeper reefs are swept by light currents and are alive with magnificent sponges and sea fans.

There are many wrecks around Lae and it has become popular diving for military buffs. The wrecks also attract unusual fish, like various pipefish and lionfish. Lae was the scene of a major WWII battle and there are remnants both on land and in the sea.

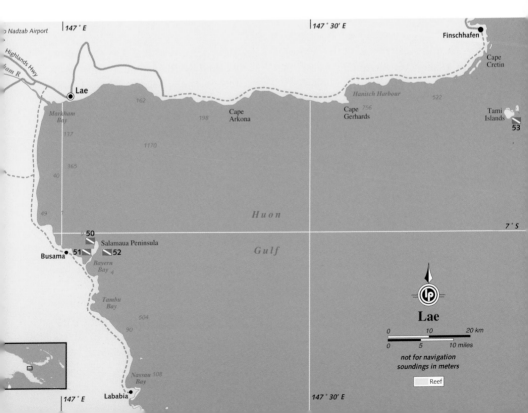

50 Salamaua Peninsula

It is possible to make day trips from Lae to dive Salamaua and nearby reefs. However, it is more convenient to make the journey as part of a weekend or longer trip, using accommodations at Salamaua or on a live-aboard. The Salamaua Peninsula provides sheltered diving all year.

Location: Salamaua Peninsular

Depth Range: 5-40m (16-130ft) plus

Access: Boat

Expertise Rating: Novice

The fringing reef around the coast has good hard corals, some soft corals. Some sites—like **The Beacon**—are popular with beginners or night divers. There is a good variety of marine life, particularly in the shallows.

The broken-up WWII wreck of the *Kotoko Maru* rests from shallow water down to 20m on the southeast side of the peninsula. The wreck is particularly interesting because of the way the coral reef has reclaimed it; some parts are now hard to identify as they have been engulfed by the vibrant reef. This is a good spot for snorkelers as well as divers, but is not accessible in southeast winds.

Near the eastern end of the peninsula are a couple of intermediate reefs that

Squirrelfish are active at night.

occur in deeper water. At **The Aquarium** and **Sheila's Reef**, you'll find lush growths of gorgonians, barrel sponges and black coral, decorated with crinoids of myriad colors.

A current usually flows over these sites and, as a consequence, they are visited by pelagics, such as dogtooth tuna and Spanish mackerel. These big fish are accompanied by good populations of resident reef fish. The Aquarium has depths up to 27m and Sheila's Reef to 20m. Both dives are usually done as drift dives to avoid anchor damage and so divers can drift with the current.

BOB HALSTEAD

A regal angelfish swims by The Aquarium.

51 *Yokohama Maru*

Near Salamaua Harbour on the western side of the peninsula lies the magnificent wreck of the *Yokohama Maru*. This upright and intact wreck is sheltered for most of the year and usually has excellent visibility and minimal currents. It sounds ideal until you find out the minimum depth is 55m to the top of the bridge. Only techincal divers trained in deep diving should attempt to explore this wreck.

For experienced deep divers this is a great dive to see a large Japanese WWII freighter. The wreck was well picked over by souvenir hunters and salvage divers before all WWII wrecks were protected in PNG.

Now it is covered by silver polyp black coral trees and white soft coral giving it a stunning, memorable and ghostly effect.

The ship is usually marked with buoys, which should not be used as moorings except by dinghies. Several dives are necessary to explore this wreck.

Location: Salamaua Harbour

Depth: 55m (180ft) plus

Access: Boat

Expertise Rating: Advanced

Ghostly appearance of the Yokohama Maru.

52 **Salamaua Offshore Reefs**

Two offshore reefs, **Shepparton Shoals** and **Benalla Banks**, lie about 8km to the southeast and northeast, respectively, of Salamaua. Shepparton Shoal is shallow on top reaching down to 7m and Benalla

Location: Off Salamaua Peninsula

Depth Range: 7-40m (23-130ft) plus

Access: Boat

Expertise Rating: Advanced

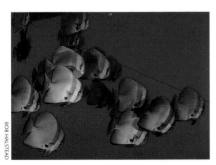

Schooling batfish at Benalla Banks.

Banks are deeper with a minimum depth of 18m. Both sites have great diving with walls, good coral growth and plenty of fish and shark life, although there are also some barren patches.

Between Lae and Salamaua is **Halfway Reef**. This deeper reef drops to 25m and, since the reef is not charted, local knowledge and an echo sounder are required to find it. It is certainly well worth a visit, being the best reef dive close to Lae. Giant barrel sponges are a feature of the reef, which also has large colorful soft corals, sea fans, clack corals and some dramatic overhangs festooned with soft corals. Fish life is excellent and sightings of whale sharks are reported regularly.

53 Tami Islands

Another cruising destination is to the Tami Islands, which have some fine diving including reefs with many sea fans, sea whips and orange elephant ear sponges.

Several particularly good reefs off the northern side of the islands rise to 5m or so for convenient anchorage and then slope to deeper water. Gradual slopes are more common here than walls, but are covered with lush growths and many fish. Choose sites receiving current for the maximum fish life.

Location: 90km east of Lae

Depth Range: 5-40m (16-130ft) plus

Access: Live-aboard

Expertise Rating: Intermediate

A sheltered lagoon suitable for night anchorage is available for boaters with local knowledge and vessels with shallow draft (less than 1.8m). The villagers are famous for their fine carved wooden bowls, which they will bring out to sell in the lagoon.

BOB HALSTEAD

A visit to the Tami Islands features excellent diving and some of the largest sponges in PNG.

Madang Dive Sites

Busy, clean and colorful. That is the first impression one gets of this tropical resort town on PNG's north shore.

Trees full of noisy fruit bats, a landscaped drive along the deep, blue ocean and parks with lily ponds that flash signs warning of crocodiles distinguish Madang from any other tropical paradise. It is as popular as it is pretty, being a major visitor destination for those wanting to relax, dive, swim or golf.

Madang is convenient for travelers as Air Niugini has one to four daily flights out of Port Moresby to Madang's conveniently located airport.

Weather Conditions

WIND: Madang experiences little seasonal variation in winds. Mornings are typically calm with sea breezes from the northeast or east in the afternoons. Easterly winds are more common during the trade wind season from May through November.

RAIN: Madang has rain year round, however it does have a distinct dry season in June through October.

WATER TEMPERATURE: Varies from average lows of 27°C (81°F) during July up to average highs of 29°C (84°F) during January/February.

People-watching can be a major pastime here. Highlanders and lowlanders mix as they decorate the streets in their varied garb. The women's bilum bags are often works of art. Slung across the back with the straps supported by the forehead, the bags hold fruits, vegetables, pottery and babies.

The town market is always busy and full of crafts, fruits and other bargains. Roasted bags of peanuts for only 10 toea help stave off the munchies. Fresh coconuts are great for drinking and bananas provide a sweet helping of potassium. Lofty ironwood trees around the Market Square are full of flying foxes that make the air come alive with their calls. At dusk they

TIM ROCK

Freshly cooked salted peanuts sold at the Madang market make a great snack.

move to the west to feed, filling the sky with a dracula-esque image. It is amazing to watch this eerie nightly migration.

The big news around Madang in 1998 was the filming of the movie *Robinson Crusoe* with actor Pierce Brosnan heading the cast. Thousands of locals took part as extras or worked in some way on the adventure film.

Other popular sites include vintage plane wrecks near the old WWII Japanese runway, which has a breathtaking overlook of the peninsula from the Lutheran grounds. Also worthwhile is a visit to one of the unique villages where pottery is handmade and fired in village ovens. This pottery is known throughout the region and people travel from afar to trade goods and foods for the prized red clay vessels.

Most of Madang's hotels are well-situated so guests can enjoy a cool evening drink along the shoreline or under the stars. A cockatoo or a furry cuscus may appear in the trees.

Madang Diving

A giant, white Coastwatchers Memorial, dedicated to those who served during the war, marks the entrance to Madang's main harbor. This monument also acts as a navigational beacon to Sek Island. A large, protected inner lagoon runs north, while the outer barrier reef is dotted with islands. There are many fine pass dives, reef dives and wrecks in this broad and beautiful area.

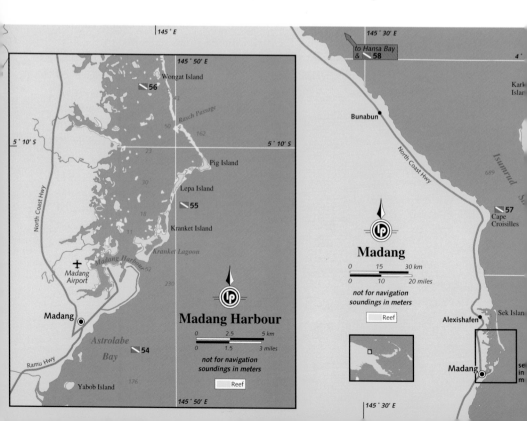

TIM ROCK

White sulphur springs near the Madang cliffs.

Divers can expect to see a great variety of fish life in the Madang region. The barrier reef contains lots of pocks and crevices that are excellent for fish development and habitat. The passes constantly channel nutrients in and out with the tides, attracting all forms of sea life up and down the food chain.

People see the undersea wonders in two ways. They either use land-based dive operations like those located at the Madang Resort or Jais Aben, or they take to a live-aboard. Live-aboards offer flexibility, platforms for night dives and can venture to far distant islands like Bagabag or the volcanic cones of Karkar.

More of these wild, offshore islands are being explored and the pelagic life is truly remarkable. In all there are 45 islands in Madang Province, three of which are still active volcanoes.

Madang Dive Sites

	Good Snorkeling	Novice	Intermediate	Advanced
54 Planet Rock	●		●	
55 Madang Outer Reefs	●			●
56 Madang Harbour Wrecks	●	●		
57 North Coast Road	●			●
58 Hansa Bay & Laing Island	●		●	

54 Planet Rock

One of the best dive sites accessible from Madang is Planet Rock, a seamount rising from very deep water to just 4m. The reeftop is small and can easily be circumnavigated. It is shown on the chart about 7km south of the entrance to Madang Harbour. The surface waters in the area are sometimes affected by run-off from rivers ashore—enough to make seeing the reef difficult. However, a few meters down, the water usually clears.

Being exposed, the reef can only be dived in calm weather and even then a current often runs over it. This just serves to enhance the fish action on the reef, which can be formidable.

The sloping pinnacle has lots of active fish life and a huge variety of anemones. The mainland end of the reef near the mooring buoy is an excellent fishwatching spot with schools of large barracuda, jacks, gilded triggerfish, snappers and plenty of smaller reef fish. Concentrate

Location: South of harbor entrance

Depth Range: 4-40m (13-130ft) plus

Access: Boat

Expertise Rating: Intermediate

on this end of the reef for lots of action. There is also a crevice that has plenty of fish life near the action point.

Yellow trumpetfish at Planet Rock.

55 Madang Outer Reefs

The most popular dive in the harbor is **Magic Passage**, named for the magical dives you can experience when conditions are right. This reef pass between Kranket and Lepa Islands comes alive when the tidal current flows in from the open sea. The pass has a sandy bottom at about 35m, which drops away steeply at the entrance. In clear conditions it is possible to sit in the pass and observe the walls on either side, covered with big barrel sponges and green tree corals.

On the bottom near the entrance are several coral rocks beautifully decorated with sea fans, soft corals and sea whips. Sweetlips line up on the bottom facing

Location: Passes entering harbor

Depth Range: 5-40m (16-130ft)

Access: Boat

Expertise Rating: Advanced

the incoming tide, while schools of bigeye trevally and barracuda whirl around above them. Sharks are sometimes seen, and many other reef creatures are found in the shallows on either side of the pass.

The site should be avoided when the tides flow out of the lagoon, as the visi-

Sweetlips have loose, rubbery lips to suck up worms and molluscs from the sea floor.

bility decreases and the fish life leaves the entrance. Look for cuttlefish in the shallow waters and in between sea whips.

Pig Island on the outer barrier reef has several interesting nearby dives and is a lovely site for anchoring and picnics. The shallow sheltered water on the lagoon side of the reef is also ideal for snorkelers.

Barracuda Point on the eastern side of the island is one of the best dives and never fails to produce good sightings of barracuda, sea perch, trevally, and other large fish.

Pig Passage on the southwest side of the island can be tricky in conditions of strong current. In more usual conditions of slight currents, the white sand of the passage brightens the many shallow reef

patches, smothered with vibrant hard and soft corals and colorful fish, including the elusive leaf scorpionfish.

North of Pig Island is **Rasch Passage**, also well worth diving. Again an incoming tide is preferable and it is worth spending some time on the front face of the drop-off near the entrance to the passage before drifting along its length. Huge barrel sponges are common here.

A tomato clownfish flits about the knobby coral.

56 | Madang Harbour Wrecks

Keep north and you'll find the lovely Wongat Island. Here, on a sandy slope on the lagoon side of the island, the old iron

Location: North Madang lagoon

Depth Range: 12-30m (40-100ft)

Access: Boat

Expertise Rating: Novice

The *Henry Leith* sinking off Wongat Island.

tug boat *Henry Leith* sits upright in 20m. This is a simple and attractive wreck dive. Soft coral growth covers the wreck and lionfish are abundant. The beautiful lacy scorpionfish is also occasionally found on the wreck.

Just a couple hundred meters away lies a magnificent **B25 Mitchell** aircraft, ditched in WWII after losing its port engine to Japanese gunfire. This wreck, first dived in 1979, lies on the slope of a small lagoon reef with its port wing tip in only 12m. Most of the guns are still visible and, apart from the port engine, the wreck is intact and covered with sea fans, sponges and soft corals. There is a very large sea fan covering the tail area. The cloth from the tail has deteriorated, leaving only the frame. The upper reef near

BOB HALSTEAD

Tail gun of the B25 Mitchell.

Wreck Diving

Wreck diving can be safe and fascinating. Penetration of shipwrecks, however, is a skilled specialty and should not be attempted without proper training. Wrecks are often unstable; they can be silty, deep and disorienting. Use an experienced guide to view wrecks and the amazing coral communities that have developed on them.

the plane is also a good place to find invertebrates.

Another remarkable wreck dive in Madang Harbour, north of Pig Island is the *Coral Queen*. This was sunk as a dive site and rests upright with its deck at 24m. The wreck has been taken over by a huge colony of flashlight fish that, on dark nights, produce so much light that divers can turn off their lights and still see the wreck. The new digital video cameras can actually capture this unusual sight on tape. The visibility, as for most dives inside the lagoon, is variable but typically 15-25m in good conditions.

57　North Coast Road

Day trips along the North Coast Road to Cape Croissilles feature several excellent dives that can be made directly from the shore.

During the southeast trade wind season when waves break on the sharp coral rocks south of the Cape, exiting the water can be difficult. Also beware of strong currents running along the shore from the south or east. Since access to these sites requires entry to traditionally owned land, it is necessary to obtain permission from the land owners. A small fee may apply.

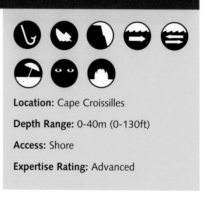

Location: Cape Croissilles

Depth Range: 0-40m (0-130ft)

Access: Shore

Expertise Rating: Advanced

In fine conditions you can dive the **Quarry** and the wreck of the **USS** *Boston* on the southern side of the Cape.

A diver looks inside the USS *Boston*.

The USS *Boston* sunk while she was engaged in mine-clearing operations just after WWII. The slice in the hull that caused her demise is clearly visible at the port stern near where the propellers—long since salvaged—became tangled in the clearing wires. The wreck lies upright with its deck is at about 30m and its bow pointing north.

A cunning way to dive the wreck making use of the prevailing current is to descend to 30m upon entry and then drift effortlessly along the reef until you encounter the wreck's stern. Using the wreck to shelter you from the current, you can explore from stern to bow. Instead of trying to swim back against the current, make the short swim across the current back to the reef slope, ascend to 5m then return south to the entry point along the reef.

By turning left right after your beach entry, you'll reach the Quarry's near vertical ridge, which descends into very deep water, has wonderful growths of soft corals, sea fans, whips and excellent fish life, including a resident school of batfish and a lone tiger shark.

This is an attractive wreck dive with lots of coral growth and usually very clear water with visibility in excess of 40m. Pelagics are seen, as well as the usual reef fish.

Lush greenery surrounds the sheltered lagoon at the Waterhole.

If weather makes access to the Quarry and USS *Boston* dangerous, drive a few kilometers farther, rounding Cape Croissilles to the **Waterhole** (also known as the "Hole in the Wall"), an easy and unique dive. Enter from a palm-fringed beach into the small, and perfectly sheltered lagoon. As you descend, a wide arch opens through the reef barrier, bottoming out at 6m and enabling divers to swim through to the open ocean and drop-off. Navigate carefully to ensure safe return to the arch for exit.

Adventurous divers can enter the water 500m or so east of the Waterhole at the **Blowhole**. Just a couple of meters from shore, the bottom drops away to a vertical wall, well covered with sponges and long sea whips. Drifting with the current, you may encounter pelagics, sharks and turtles before ending up at the Waterhole for an easy exit. However, beware! The current has been known to change without warning and instead of an easy drift, you can find yourself fighting to get to the Waterhole.

This is a beautiful area for diving and the water is invariably very clear. There is also good snorkeling in the Waterhole.

58 Hansa Bay & Laing Island

In as little as four hours (in dry season), you can drive the 230km along the North Coast Road from Madang to Hansa Bay. Here a fleet of Japanese freighters was caught and bombed by U.S. forces during WWII. The bombing left many shipwrecks—and a few aircraft wrecks—on the relatively shallow bottom.

The site could be a wreck divers' paradise if not for the unpredictable visibility in Hansa Bay, depending on both local

Location: Hansa Bay

Depth Range: 0-24m (0-79ft)

Access: Live-aboard

Expertise Rating: Intermediate

rainfall and seasonal currents. The best season is from May through November, although it is possible to get good diving at other times.

The most commonly dived wreck in Hansa Bay is the *Sushi Maru*, which lies 500m from the beach in front of Nubia village. This large freighter—over 5000 tons—sits upright and even has trucks and a fire engine in one of its holds. The bridge and superstructure have broken-up, but the main attraction of the wreck is its incredible amount of marine growth. A huge variety of corals and sponges harbor innumerable marine creatures. Australian naturalist Neville Coleman once declared he could run a

BOB HALSTEAD

A truck rests in the *Sushi Maru's* cargo hold.

complete marine biology course just on the foredeck of the wreck.

With a maximum depth of 24m, and shallowest only 4m, this wreck can be thoroughly explored. Be careful of deteriorating steel plates when any swim-throughs are planned.

The *Davit* Wreck can be spotted at low tide northeast of the river mouth near Sisimango. This wreck is interesting though it does not sport as much marine growth as the *Sushi Maru*. Off its stern lies the remains of a twin-screw wooden boat. The wood was long ago eaten by marine worms. The brass fittings on the engines get polished by turtles seeking shelter.

The **Mast Head** wreck lies nearby to the south. An American **Air Cobra** aircraft wreck lies in 27m a little farther offshore. In all, there are reported to be 34 wrecks of ships, boats and aircraft in the bay, and quite a few remain undived.

In the middle of Hansa Bay is **Laing Island**, the site of the King Leopold III Biological Research Station. Permission is required to visit the island, but visitors are usually welcome.

There is some good easy diving around the island's fringing reef, particularly on the eastern side where the reef drops to deep water. The more sheltered western side has a sloping reef with good coral growth and a barge wreck in 5m.

Offshore of Laing Island are a series of seldom dived seamounts offering dynamic reef diving. **Encounter Reef** starts at 5m and rapidly plummets deeply on the northeast side. Sharks are common. As may be expected the reef is visited by many large pelagic species and a resident school of barracuda. Soft corals and sea fans are scattered among the excellent hard coral growths and giant clams sometimes dot the reeftop.

The Mast Head Wreck in Hansa Bay.

Kimbe Bay Dive Sites

TIM ROCK

Sunrise over Kimbe Bay

Kimbe Bay is on the north side of New Britain Island between the Willaumez Peninsula and Lolobau Island. The flight into Hoskins airport is a memorable one. Volcanic peaks, still puffing steam and smoke, jut above lush rainforest. Closer to sea level, large plantations of oil palms and copra coconut trees line the highway.

On the drive from the airport into Kimbe town, birdsong and the single-lane bridges are reminders that this is still wild and rural territory, even though Kimbe is considered a major seaport for northern New Britain.

Kimbe is near the ocean but is fairly unassuming. Small hotels, stores and restaurants mingle with houses, and a produce market sits at the edge of town. A large sports field draws people from all over the region to watch local matches or an occasional visit from another country's football team.

Up the road from Kimbe is Talasea. The Walindi Plantation dive lodge sits between the two cities. Outdoor activities abound in this region. Try mountain bike riding through the palms and into the hills via logging roads, or visiting the thermal streams and small geysers, where a good soaking does wonders for aches and pains. The bird life is remarkable in this jungle setting.

Near Walindi is Mahonia na Dari, a research and conservation center partly funded by The Nature Conservancy. It works to protect both the marine and terrestrial diversity in the Kimbe Bay and Willaumez Peninsula. During one survey of this rich bay, 860 species of fish fauna were found, including three newly described species. The study also counted nearly 350 species of stony corals, excluding soft corals, gorgonians and black coral.

Weather Conditions

WIND: If strong, the southeast trade winds from May through November sometimes funnel between volcanoes on New Britain Island, but the bay is usually calm. From January through March the bay is exposed to northwesterly winds.

RAIN: Kimbe's distinct wet season falls between January and March.

WATER TEMPERATURE: Varies from average lows of 28°C (82°F) during June/July up to average highs of 30°C (86°F) during January/February.

Kimbe Bay Diving

Kimbe diving features unique seamounts capped with coral towers rising to the surface through exceptionally clear water. The towers are alive with creatures big and small and the seascapes, decorated with red sea whips, giant pink sea fans, huge barrel and elephant ear sponges, are a favorite for many of the world's top underwater photographers.

Local operators have taken considerable effort to keep these reefs as pristine as possible. Most are affixed with moorings and are well maintained. This, coupled with educational programs and constant contact with the shore villages, has ensured that the reefs are as spectacular as when first explored in the early 1980s.

Whales, orcas and dolphins are commonly encountered in the bay, and smaller reef creatures are abundant. Outside the bay more islands and reefs, also of superb quality, are easily accessible from a live-aboard.

Sea whips stretch tall on Kimbe Bay's unique seamounts.

Kimbe Bay Dive Sites

	Good Snorkeling	Novice	Intermediate	Advanced
59 Walindi Reefs	●	●		
60 Schumann & Restorf Islands	●	●		
61 Joy's Reef & Charmaine's Reef	●	●		
62 Kimbe Bay Reef Chain	●		●	
63 Kimbe Bay Seamounts	●			●
64 Kimbe Island Bommie	●			●
65 Hoskins Reefs & Wulai Island	●			●
66 Bali Vitu Islands				●
67 Lolobau Island Offshore Reefs	●			●

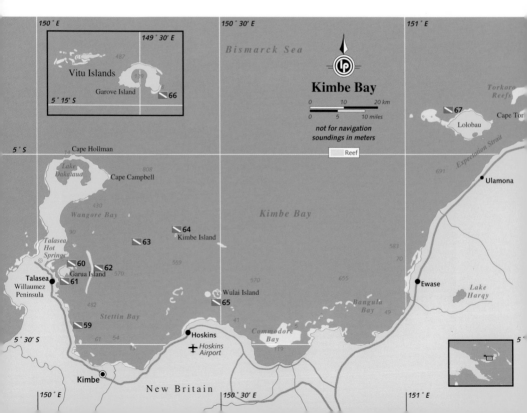

59 | Walindi Reefs

The area is blessed with mostly calm seas. Even in windy conditions, you can find sheltered dive sites close to the Walindi Resort. The **Hanging Gardens** and **Numundo Reef** are two sites just a few minutes from the resort that are always accessible and offer a multitude of small reef creatures and fish.

The Hanging Gardens features a vertical wall falling from the surface to about 27m, with numerous ledges and overhangs. Long sponge growths dangle from the wall, often with clinging crinoids. This is an excellent site for night diving—the mooring is just a couple of minutes from the Walindi dock and the wall's many cracks and crevices shelter a collection of odd and colorful invertebrates.

Location: Walindi Resort

Depth Range: 1-27m (3-89ft)

Access: Boat

Expertise Rating: Novice

Night life includes flashlight fish, nudibranchs and live shells—look for the beautiful file shell below 18m.

Numundo Reef has a shallow staghorn coral garden, which slopes away to deeper water where lionfish swim among the coral bommies. Look for small aggregations of the lovely filamentous wrasse.

The tree-covered grounds of the Walindi Plantation Resort.

Flashlightfish have an organ under their eyes that contains luminous bacteria.

60 | Schumann & Restorf Islands

Schumann Island and Restorf Island offer sheltered diving and an abundance of the more unusual creatures found on sandy bottoms near coral reefs.

Both islands are favorite lunch spots. Native pigeons live on the islands, along with hawks and sea eagles. The constant, eerie cooing of the pigeons adds to the islands' mystery and unusual beauty.

Location: 22km (14 miles) north of Walindi

Depth Range: 4-35m (13-115ft)

Access: Boat

Expertise Rating: Novice

At Schumann Island, panda clownfish and their attendant porcelain crabs are easy to spot on sand anemones, which will retract into the sand when disturbed. The shallows can provide great surprises and should not be ignored. Observant divers will notice sand divers, curious wormfish, shrimp gobies and banded pipefish. There are also some interesting lava formations on Schumann.

Restorf Island has excellent diving and snorkeling. An idyllic beach surrounds towering, jungled rock spires. The northeast side has a rich channel with huge sea fans, elephant ear sponges in hues of yellow, pink and tan. A nice stand of lettuce corals has a couple of brilliant blue ribbon eels living nearby.

Grey reef sharks are reported here and you'll have a good chance of seeing larger fish including the occasional manta ray. Look near the white sandy patches for the spiny devilfish, camouflaged as it moves along the bottom with modified pectoral fins. Mantis shrimp and rare garden eels are also found along the bottom. The northeast wall has gorgonians and black coral in shallow water.

Titan triggerfish, which seasonally nest in the sand patches, form large craters by turning on their sides and finning furiously. Be warned! Titan triggerfish will defend their eggs against all intruders and have been known to inflict painful bites on divers.

TIM ROCK

Restorf Island is popular with snorkelers.

TIM ROCK

Elephant ear sponges make dramatic photos.

61 Joy's Reef & Charmaine's Reef

Just a couple of kilometers south/southeast of Restorf Island is a small patch reef that offers good macrophotography opportunities. Joy's Reef is exposed at low tide, with a natural swimming pool at its center. The reef slopes away but is bounded by a small but sheer wall before reaching the sand bottom at 24-35m.

Location: Near Restorf Island

Depth Range: 0-35m (0-115ft)

Access: Boat

Expertise Rating: Novice

The eastern wall is particularly lush and well worth a careful search for small marine critters. On the sand are isolated coral bommies with sponges and gorgonians. At the base of the wall the sand hosts pairs of the exotic crab-eyed goby, with its distinctive twin "eyespots" on its dorsal fin. Look in the sandy rubble for unique nudibranchs.

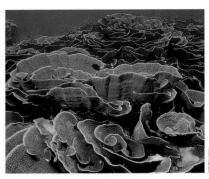

Cabbage corals grow in the sandy outcrops.

Charmaine's Reef is a beautifully landscaped site with a loaf-shaped, coral-covered reeftop and a deep finger starting at 23m and sloping to 34m. Look for reef sharks here. There are the trademark sea whips, red whips and large gorgonian fans found along the reef.

Snorkelers and underwater photographers will marvel at the large clownfish community found in shallow water. Three clown damsel species mingle here, providing lots of shallow water entertainment.

Crab-eyed goby on Joy's Reef.

62 | Kimbe Bay Reef Chain

Three kilometers or so to the east of Restorf Island is a curved reef chain, running roughly north/south. This chain marks the edge of the continental shelf where the bottom abruptly plunges to 500m or more.

Donna's Reef to the south is the first in the chain. The big feature of this dive is two shallow coral areas reaching to just below the surface. They are surrounded by a staghorn coral garden on one side and a plate coral garden on the other. This is a beautiful, cascading formation and the gardens are full of small fish.

Macrophotographers can carefully search for exquisite shrimp and tiny white pipefish. Lionfish like the northeast end of this bommie and squarespot anthias are found below the mooring at 18m.

Location: Reefs east of Restorf Island

Depth Range: 1-40m (3-130ft) plus

Access: Boat

Expertise Rating: Intermediate

Christine's Reef has some lovely seascapes, particularly at a saddle between the main reef and two smaller, detached reefs. Descending over an expanse of staghorn coral, you'll reach the saddle, easily recognized by for its sea fans, sea whips and barrel sponges covered with crinoids. Sea anemones are common on this reef and photogenic longnose hawkfish can be found in the sea fans. There is

TIM ROCK

Consistent currents mean healthy soft corals.

for razorfish and a pair of trumpetfish living in the whips. Large sea fans are found all along this wall and percula clownfish are regulars here. On the eastern side there is a sheer wall, and to the north, on the western side, a sloping hard coral garden. The staghorn coral in the shallows provides very good snorkeling.

BOB HALSTEAD

Feather stars make great photographic subjects.

excellent snorkeling on this reef, which is only 1m deep in places.

Kirsty Jayne's Reef starts a little deeper at 4m but the best diving is to be found at 18m where soft corals, sea fans and whips form a colorful coral garden. Spinecheeked anemonefish and the unusual shrimpfish, which is paper thin and swims head down among the sea whips, inhabit the reef. Look for the ornately colored mandarinfish here when the sun is getting low, as it is most commonly encountered at dusk.

The next reef in the chain is **Vanessa's Reef** and this is much deeper, with its shallowest part at 18m. The reef is a ridge featuring large orange elephant ear sponges and the usual sea fans, sea whips, and barrel sponges. Dives can be made to 35m and when a current is running, there's a good chance of seeing grey reef sharks or a school of barracuda.

Susan's Reef is home to a pair of longfin bannerfish, which have become preferred and cooperative subjects for many international photographers. Susan's is usually dived at 22m at the southern end, where there are particularly dense growths of red sea whips. Look

Katherine's Reef is small enough to be easily circumnavigated on a single dive. Anemones and their fish are common. See if you can spot the five different species of anemonefish. At a sand and rubble slope at 22m on the northern side, the brilliant redlined sea cucumber—by far the most photogenic of the usually dull sea cucumber family—can be found with careful searching.

BOB HALSTEAD

Red-lined sea cucumber at Katherine's Reef.

63 Kimbe Bay Seamounts

Unique to Kimbe Bay are a series of seamounts capped with coral towers and surrounded by deep water, yet only an hour's boat ride from a land-based dive resort. On a clear day, you can see the the seamounts from the plane when flying into Hoskins airport. Some of these reefs are very shallow—virtually awash at low tide—while others peak 20m below the surface.

Inglis Shoal, just over 30km north/ northeast of Walindi, has 12m of water over its shallowest part. It slopes away dramatically, becoming vertical in places. When diving deeper than 30m, this is a good site to see scalloped hammerhead sharks and larger pelagics. A school of barracuda is often spotted in shallower water along with masses of other reef fish, particularly if a slight current is running.

The reeftop has a good cover of grey soft corals that obscure much of the hard coral growth. Look for the odd behavior of the batfish here, which swim sideways and parallel to the reef into the current. They may also follow you up to the boat.

A few kilometers north of Inglis Shoal is the famous Ema Reef, one of the most scenic of all the seamounts. This reef is

Location: Offshore in Kimbe Bay

Depth Range: 1-40m (3-130ft) plus

Access: Boat

Expertise Rating: Advanced

divided into two major dive sites, **South Ema** and **North Ema**.

North Ema is only under 1m of water. Divers should descend from the shallow main reef down a deep saddle to a bommie whose top is at 35m. The bommie is covered with sea fans, sea whips and colorful soft corals. From the deep water surrounding the bommie, hammerheads sometimes appear.

South Ema is reached by diving down another deep saddle from the shallow reef to a bommie that rises to 10m. This

Typical thriving scenery at Ema's Reef.

Magnificent balled anemones come in many different hues.

BOB HALSTEAD
A hawksbill turtle visits South Ema.

features a beautiful swim-through at about 30m, where the western side of the saddle starts to rise again. There are prolific growths of gorgonians and sponges and a very good population of reef fish. Schooling jacks and barracudas are common. Macrophotographers will enjoy the clingfish, crinoid crabs and yellowtip anemone shrimp. Snorkelers will enjoy

the beautiful coral gardens in the shallows and may even see turtles.

South Bay Reef is a one-hour fast boat ride north/northeast from Walindi. The northern side of the reef drops vertically and the wall has stunning growths of lace coral at about 18m. Silvertip sharks are often seen deeper, but the whole reef is vibrant and well worth a visit.

To the east is a deeper reef called **Bradford Shoal**, starting at about 20m. This reef has twin peaks sloping down to a lip at about 27m, becoming almost vertical. The reeftop has some large plate corals and, being deeper, is good for finding some of the less common reef fish, such as Burgess's butterflyfish, blackspot angelfish and harlequin grouper. Schools of bigeye trevally, barracuda, rainbow runners and batfish mill around on the reeftop.

64 Kimbe Island Bommie

Almost directly northeast of Walindi Plantation Resort (about one hour in a fast boat) you'll find Kimbe Island, which is marked by a navigational beacon. The island is surrounded by shallow reef and makes an excellent

Location: Near Kimbe Island

Depth Range: 27-40m (90-130ft) plus

Access: Boat

Expertise Rating: Advanced

BOB HALSTEAD

picnic spot after diving the Kimbe Island Bommie.

This is another deep dive with a deep minimum depth. The underwater scenery features an abundance of soft corals and gorgonians. With a slight current running, this can be one of the most action-packed dives in Kimbe Bay. There are large schools of fish and plenty of pelagics. This is another site regularly visited by spinner dolphins.

65 Hoskins Reefs & Wulai Island

Location: Near Hoskins Peninsula

Depth Range: 1-40m (3-130ft) plus

Access: Boat

Expertise Rating: Advanced

Paluma Reef, only a couple of kilometers off the Hoskins Peninsula, is notable for its soft corals. The dive is a deep underwater bommie at 22m, joined to a main reef by a descending ridge at 25-33m. Sea fans and sea whips are scattered among the soft corals, creating a top spot for wide-angle photography.

Reeson Reefs is only an 8-minute cruise from Hoskins. The best dive here is the northeast corner where a sloping reef is covered in hard corals. Abundant barrel sponges are dressed in a colorful array of crinoids. The fish life over the slope is healthy and includes schools of barracuda, batfish, trevally and surgeonfish. A pod of spinner dolphins makes its home in the lagoon.

Robert's Reef is only 4km offshore from the Hoskins airport. The northwest corner of this square-shaped reef is a long undulating ridge that starts near the surface. It dips to 33m before ending in a plateau crested with hard corals in 22m. The most marine life is found on the descending part of the ridge and on the plateau. A great variety of fish swim around the soft corals, black coral and gorgonians. The sea fans here are spec-

Razorfish live in the red sea whips.

tacular. On your return ascent up the slope between 12m and 3m, you can find seven species of anemonefish in six different species of anemones.

Agu Reef to the north of Hoskins, about 12km offshore, is another worthy reef dive, particularly as sharks are

Fish life is abundant around Hoskin's Peninsula, including this resident school of jacks

commonly seen on the southern point deeper than 20m. This reef has predominantly hard corals in superb, pristine condition and you'll find excellent small fish life.

The distinctive **Wulai Island** is a miniature atoll complete with a circular barrier reef. The lagoon has sheltered diving in windy conditions, but the best diving is in the passes. The southeast pass is particularly interesting, featuring some beautiful and very large barrel sponges.

Wulai Island is about 9km north of Hoskins and has a large reef to its west, outside the lagoon.

Giant barrel sponges near Wulai Island.

66 Bali Vitu Islands

Garove Island, 60km northeast of the northern tip of the Willaumez Peninsula is yet another surprising and magical places.

Once a large volcano, ancient explosions have breached the southern caldera of **Garove Island**. The cone was flooded by water over 300m deep. Ships can sail into the cone through the narrow south pass, surrounded by the steep caldera walls—a perfect harbor except for the extremely deep water.

A small island inside the caldera has some shallow reef but the coral is poor-

Location: Northeast of Willaumez Peninsula

Depth Range: 8-40m (26-130ft) plus

Access: Live-Aboard

Expertise Rating: Advanced

ly formed, lacking the water movement essential for lush growth. Also villagers reported seeing a large crocodile in 1992, which must have swum all the way from the mainland. It is the diving outside the caldera that makes the island worth visiting.

Lama Shoal is one of the best reefs in the area, 2km off the southeast side of Garove. This small reef rises to 8m and slopes away steeply on all sides. The slopes are covered with prolific growths of black coral, gorgonians and barrel sponges, and the reef supports an enormous array of fish life. A large school of

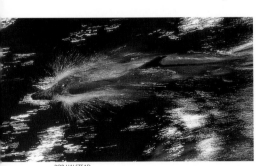

BOB HALSTEAD
Spinner dolphins play near the surface.

barracuda is resident. Bigeye trevally zoom in towards visiting divers, dogtooth tuna and sharks constantly patrol, and schools of reef fish and fusiliers abound.

Something else makes this reef unusual: the reeftop is covered with a blanket of the small olive-colored anemone-like creatures called Corallimorpharians. Beware of these and keep well clear.

67 Lolobau Island Offshore Reefs

On the eastern side of Kimbe Bay near Lolobau Island are several series of reefs, too far from Kimbe to allow comfortable day diving but in easy range of liveaboards.

The isolated **Fairway Reef** is about 20km offshore and 20km southwest of Lolobau. The main reef is separated from a small bommie by a ridge, which has a few colorful sea fans, but the small bommie is the place for the best fish action. A school of barracuda is a reliable sight and sharks are common.

Father Reef, 26km due west of Lolobau, is actually a hook-shaped reef chain, offering some very good diving. Favorite sites include **Father's Arch**, reached by swimming down a ridge where the arch tops at 25m and is full of soft corals, gorgonians and excellent fish life.

Jayne's Gully is a dynamic dive in a deep channel between two reefs. Soft corals and sea fans grow on either side of the channel; sharks and schools of fish often parade through it depending on the current.

Location: South of harbor entrance

Depth Range: 5-40m (16-130ft) plus

Access: Live-aboard

Expertise Rating: Advanced

BOB HALSTEAD

Sea fans adorned with crinoids at Fairway Reef.

Other reefs well worth exploring are the **Banban Reefs** and islands off the northwest side of Lolobau, and the **Torkoro Reefs** east of Lolobau. The Torkoro Reefs have limited good shallow coral cover, but the coral improves dramatically deeper than 8m. The reasons for this are not clear though it could be that freshwater from nearby rivers damages the shallow corals in times of heavy rainfall. Regardless, for most of the year the visiblity is very clear, rarely dropping below 50m.

TIM ROCK

Colorful soft coral.

Rabaul Dive Sites

Weather Conditions

WIND: Wind conditions have little effect on diving, although certain sites may be unsettled in rare strong wind conditions.

RAIN: Varies only slightly throughout the year, with the driest months statistically May through November.

WATER TEMPERATURE: Varies from average lows of 28°C (82°F) during July up to average highs of 30°C (86°F) in January/February.

Many locals still talk of the September 1994 volcanic eruption of Tuvurvur, a blast that changed the face of once-bustling Rabaul. Evidence of the blast is prominent. The mount still spews ash and much of the town remains buried under ash and mud. The people of Rabaul are a resilient lot however, and haven't let a volcano get them down.

The Tuvurvur blast marked the third time this century that the town had been destroyed. A massive eruption in 1937 and bombing by Americans and Australians in WWII also leveled the place.

But that was then and this is now. While many government services and businesses are relocating to neighboring Kokopo and near the new airstrip of Tokua, Rabaul attempts to rise again. The Kaivuna, Travelodge and the Hamamas hotels have reopened after extensive renovations and tourists are coming back to see Rabaul's rebirth.

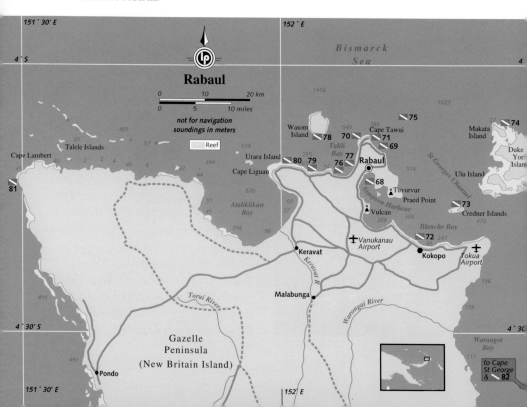

Rabaul Harbour, one of the more scenic in the Pacific, consists of the flooded caldera of an ancient and mighty volcano. Ringed with both active and dormant vents, Rabaul scenery is dramatic. The frequent earth tremors and wafting smell of sulphur are constant reminders of the town's precarious situation.

Rabaul Diving

Rabaul has some excellent reefs and specialist dives, which have boosted its reputation as a diver's destination. But the notion of diving is not new here. For years fanatical residents made nightly ventures to local beaches, diving for rare shells.

Their finds have become legendary. Local divers became professional shell collectors, feeding a thriving shell export business. Those days are gone, and the collecting of live shells is no longer allowed.

Divers these days are more interested in the amazing animals that create the shell masterpieces, and in photographing rather than killing them. The ease of shore diving into deep water also leads divers to make the pilgrimage to Rabaul.

Rabaul Dive Sites	Good Snorkeling	Novice	Intermediate	Advanced
68 Rabaul Harbour Shipwrecks				●
69 George's Wreck			●	
70 Pete Biplane Wreck	●		●	
71 Submarine Base			●	
72 Zero Fighter & Takubar Wreck			●	
73 Pigeon Islands	●		●	
74 Rainbow Reef & Heaven's Gate			●	
75 St. George's Channel Seamount				●
76 Kulau Lodge Beach Wrecks			●	
77 BP Wharf		●		
78 Watom Island	●		●	
79 Midway Reef	●		●	
80 Fringing Reefs	●	●		
81 Bangkok Pass				●
82 Baldwin's Bridge				●

68 Rabaul Harbour Shipwrecks

Like other wrecks close to the Vulcan Volcano, Rabaul's most popular shipwreck dive, the *Hakaii Maru*, was buried by the volcanic eruption. Because the volcanoes still sporadically erupt, visibility in the harbor is poor. The *Manko Maru*, *Italy Maru* and *Yamayuri Maru* can still be dived but are heavily silted.

Location: Rabaul Harbour

Depth Range: 20-40m (65-130ft) plus

Access: Boat

Expertise Rating: Advanced

The *Manko Maru* lies upright not far from the wharves and has suffered some stern damage from large ships anchoring nearby. However, at 35m, this is one of the more easily accessible shipwrecks.

The ship was originally a refrigeration vessel weighing 1,502 tons. It was sunk in November 1943, by Captain Charles W. Howe, U.S. 5th Division Air Force. A remarkable photograph of the ship sinking, with the smoke-engulfed shores in the background, appears in the book *Rabaul's Forgotten Fleet* .

The wreck is often shrouded with misty water layers, giving it a ghostly aura. Lionfish and other large scorpionfish are its principal inhabitants.

Resting on its starboard side in a battered state, the *Italy Maru* at 5,859 tons, was one of the largest ships sunk in Rabaul. The bow and the stern at 30m are still recognizable, though much of the wreck is hard to distinguish. A resident school of batfish know their way around, sometimes startling nervous divers if the visibility is poor. Experienced wreck divers can penetrate the engine room through a hole in the uppermost port side.

The 5,028-ton *Yamayuri Maru* is a deep dive, but a good one with the wreck upright and intact. The bow is at 43m and stern at 40m. This wreck also has two guns mounted on its decks, the foredeck gun having two large anchors nearby.

Looking for Lionfish

Lionfish are common in all habitats but the greatest species variety and numbers occur in sheltered areas. Five distinct species are regularly seen: feathery lionfish, *Pterois volitans*; spot-fin lionfish, *Pterois antennata*; zebra lionfish, *Dendrochirus zebra*; dwarf lionfish, *Dendrochirus brachypterus* and the eyespot lionfish, *Dendrochirus biocellatus*.

The dwarf lionfish is found in sand areas and is often associated with anemones. Eyespot lionfish are nocturnal and shy away from a diver's light.

Feathery lionfish are especially prolific on the shipwrecks, swimming about in groups of up to 10. They tend to come out in the late afternoons to feed and patrol through the night.

TIM ROCK

69 George's Wreck

Outside the Rabaul Harbour two of Rabaul's top wreck dives remain undisturbed, including George's Wreck, which hangs bow-up on a steep slope just southeast of Cape Tawui. Although it can be a beach dive, it is far more convenient to use a boat as the road stops short of the wreck site.

The bow, with the starboard anchor still firmly in the hausepipe, reaches to 15m but the stern is at 55m with the rudder and propeller buried in the sand. The water here is usually clear and a slight current sometimes runs over the wreck, attracting marine life.

The name of the ship is actually unknown. It appears to be a mine-layer as there are cable-laying rollers on the bow and wire rope in the aft hold. The wreck got its name from a Rabaul personality and adventurer, George Tyres, who was the first to dive it.

Location: South of Cape Tawui

Depth Range: 15-40m (50-130ft)

Access: Boat or shore

Expertise Rating: Intermediate

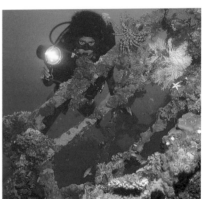

Coral-encrusted bow rail of George's Wreck.

70 Pete Biplane Wreck

The Pete Mitsubishi biplane, apparently sunk at its mooring, is in excellent condition for such a fragile aircraft. It sits upright at 27m next to the slope of the fringing reef. This reef rises to 3m and can be snorkeled—you can often see the biplane from the surface. The water along this stretch of beach is almost always crystal clear, with at least 40m visibility.

With a slight current usually running, the wreck has become decorated with soft corals and sponges, making it very photogenic. The reef slope has some good corals and offers an excellent variety of marine life for first-class snorkeling in the shallows.

Location: 1km (.6 miles) west of Tawui

Depth Range: 4-30m (13-100ft)

Access: Boat or shore

Expertise Rating: Intermediate

71 Submarine Base

At Cape Tawui there is an unusual beach dive known as the Submarine Base. The wall at this site is so steep and starts in such shallow water that Japanese submarines were able to use it as a wharf for re-provisioning. Caves were tunneled into the cliff face to provide storage for the submarine supplies.

The site is usually flat calm but a soft current flowing along the wall has

Location: East side of Cape Tawui

Depth Range: 0-40m (0-130ft) plus

Access: Shore

Expertise Rating: Advanced

Shells, like the golden cowrie, abound in Rabaul.

caused a marvelous variety of creatures to take up residence. Being deep, it is also visited by larger fish and sharks.

This is an excellent shore dive and can be easily accessed from the beach. There is a small charge for access to the site and for parking. In exchange your car will be looked after by the landowner. This is also an excellent night dive for skilled divers.

72 Zero Fighter & Takubar Wreck

Another excellent aircraft wreck is that of the classic Zero Fighter off a beach south of Rabaul on the way to Kokopo. A guide is essential to find the wreck, which you'll reach after a short swim down a descending sand bottom past scattered small coral bommies.

The wreck is at 27m, intact and upright. Its wings are flush with the sand bottom and the propeller is still in place. The open cockpit is usually full of baitfish. The water is clear. This is a good opportunity for photographers to get great pictures of one of the most famous WWII aircrafts.

While you're in the area, continue driving along the coast road through Kokopo to Takubar, 34km from Rabaul.

Location: Kokopo Road beach

Depth: 27m (89ft)

Access: Shore

Expertise Rating: Intermediate

Off another beach, the Takubar Wreck can be dived. This is probably the 4,981-ton *Kinkasan Maru*, resting on her port side, partly buried in the sand and fairly broken-up. This is an interesting dive to try and identify the various sections of the wreck. There are good coral and sponge growths on the wreck and a thriving population of fish.

73 Pigeon Islands

Between Rabaul and the island of New Ireland is the deep, blue St. George's Channel. A steady current flows through, joining the waters of the Solomon Sea to the south and the Bismark Sea to the north. For most of the year the water flows north, but January through March the current reverses. Obstructing the Channel are the Duke of York Islands and the two small Credner or "Pigeon" Islands closer to Rabaul. As might be expected, some good reef diving in very clear water can be found around these islands.

Little Pigeon (western Credner Island) has a spectacular drift dive, which ends up at the wreck of a small coastal freighter. The *Malis* was scuttled for divers in 1985. To dive Little Pigeon and the *Malis*, get into the water on the northwestern side of the island. Check the current before entering to ascertain its direction—it usually flows to the west carrying you along a near vertical wall from 1m down to 35m.

As you drift around the end of the island, the wall changes into a slope. Ascend it to 15m to the *Malis*. This pho-

Location: Between Rabaul and Duke of York Island

Depth Range: 1-35m (3-115ft)

Access: Boat

Expertise Rating: Intermediate

togenic 30m-long wreck is upright and points up the slope with a slight starboard list.

The larger and more eastern of the two islands has some good wall diving on its northwestern side. It is sheltered in the southeast season. **Rebecca's Corner** has very shallow reef on top that makes anchoring difficult. But you can descend the wall—25m is a good depth—then swim slowly along to the east through a vertical garden of soft corals and sea fans. Batfish and sharks are frequent visitors, but it is also worth searching for smaller critters, such as nudibranchs.

BOB HALSTEAD

Solar powered nudibranch.

74   Rainbow Reef & Heaven's Gate

The Duke of York Island has several very good reef dives. Rainbow Reef is to the northwest of Mait Iri Island and, as the name suggests, is a brilliantly colorful reef.

Sand gutters slice through the reef where a mixture of hard corals and gorgonians slope from 6m to 35m, followed by a series of spurs. In any slight current schooling fish hang out at the front edge of the reef. Barracuda and sharks may also pay a visit.

The opening between Mait Iri Island and the northern tip of the main Duke of York Island is called Heaven's Gate. Divers should anchor in the channel near the edge of the drop-off. After descending the channel to 10m, you'll find the bottom suddenly drops away to a deep wall. The channel has some pretty coral

Location: Duke of York Island

Depth Range: 6-35m (20-115ft)

Access: Boat

Expertise Rating: Intermediate

bommies, but you should initially head straight over the drop-off and down the wall to some magnificent stands of black coral at about 25m.

Shrimpfish and ghost pipefish are often found among the black coral branches. If the tide is flowing into the channel, you'll be mesmerized by the fish life milling around the entrance. Some of the regularly sighted larger fish include barracuda, trevally, dogtooth tuna and eagle rays. Both these dive sites typically are blessed with visibility in excess of 40m.

Black coral at Heaven's Gate.

Pipefish live in black coral branches.

75   St. George's Channel Seamount

St. George's Channel Seamount rises from deep in St. George's Channel. This tip of an ancient mountain reaches to 27m below the surface. There is no drop-off (the mount slopes away on all sides), but the top is covered with large sea fans, bushes of black coral, sea whips and barrel sponges. The area is quite large and, since there is always a swift current flowing, you

Location: 9km (6 miles) northeast of Cape Tawui

Depth Range: 27-40m (90-130ft)

Access: Boat

Expertise Rating: Advanced

must take care not to get disorientated and drift away from the boat. Larger fish, including sailfish, grey reef and silvertip sharks, often visit.

This is not a dive for the inexperienced. You should always carry a safety sausage or other signaling device. Have someone on board keep a sharp lookout from the boat. Drifting away in St. George's Channel could really spoil your day.

BOB HALSTEAD

Grey reef shark in St. George's Channel.

76   Kulau Lodge Beach Wrecks

These wrecks are reached by small boat from the beach and are marked by a buoy. The wrecks are connected by a guide rope that descends from 8m down to 35m on a gradually sloping, silty bottom.

Despite the silt, the wrecks have collected a surprising array of marine life. Visibility is usually good enough to get reasonable photographs, but be careful not to stir up the sediment. Sea turtles are commonly seen here, particularly on night dives, and dugong and shovelnose shark encounters have also been reported.

Location: Talili Bay

Depth Range: 8-35m (26-115ft)

Access: Shore

Expertise Rating: Intermediate

Part of a Japanese Zero Fighter is among the wrecks. The marking buoy is near a garden of giant clams. Juvenile red emperors are always in residence and divers with skilled eyes will also find crocodilefish and frogfish.

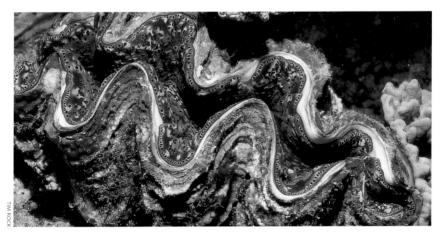

TIM ROCK

Tridacna clam nestles in the coral.

77 BP Wharf

Another interesting dive in Talili Bay and easily accessible from the Kulau Beach Resort is the BP Wharf. Permission to dive the wharf is readily granted when there are no ships due.

As it is a long-established wharf, the marine growth here is nothing short of fabulous. Visibility is not always the

Location: Talili Bay

Depth Range: 0-17m (0-55ft)

Access: Boat or Shore

Expertise Rating: Novice

Stonefish at the BP Wharf.

best but this is an incredible site for macrophotographers.

There are also genuine stonefish living here, usually in the sand at the base of the wharf in 17m. This is also an amazing night dive, but watch out for the stonefish, many lionfish and scorpionfish.

78 Watom Island

On the north side of Rabaul is Watom Island, just a few kilometers offshore from Talili Bay. The island can be dived all around its circumference, with unique underwater scenery at each site.

The eastern side is the most popular featuring **The Grotto,** a wall dive sculptured with massive cuts, caves and overhangs. A pair of Japanese barges sunk near the anchorage add interest.

The area is decorated with many small soft corals and sponges—a scenic dive and a rewarding site for wide-angle photography. The drop-off falls from near the surface to at least 75m.

North of The Grotto is **Peter's Point,** where the fringing reef forms a point. This exposed point attracts sharks, large pelagics and a multitude of reef fish. It is possible to anchor a small boat just south of the point, then swim along the edge of the vertical wall. This is an

Location: Watom Island

Depth Range: 0-40m (0-130ft) plus

Access: Boat

Expertise Rating: Intermediate

excellent place to just sit and watch the world go by.

Farther north still, at the northeast tip of Watom Island, is **Watom's Wall.** This is a classic wall dive well decorated with marine growth and with plenty of crevices to explore for invertebrates. Keep one eye looking to sea as anything could turn up here. Starting at the surface the wall drops vertically to very deep water although the best diving is in the first 30m. The Grotto, Peter's and Watom's are exposed to southeast winds, but shelter and good diving can easily be found by simply moving to the leeward side of the island.

West Point juts out on the western side of Watom and various wall dives are possible on either side of the point. Deep divers can descend the point itself, where a ledge appears at 53m and is a good spot to see if any hammerhead sharks or pelagics turn up.

On the south side of Watom is the **Garden of Fans,** a series of shallow reefs exposed to currents. The ready food supply means gorgonians thrive, and some of the many sea fans reach over 2.5m high. Divers often encounter turtles and grey reef sharks among the schools of reef fish. These sites are directly in front of villages and you should make arrangements with the villagers before diving.

BOB HALSTEAD

"Garden of Fans" is an apt name for this site, where sponges and gorgonians blossom.

79 Midway Reef

Midway Reef is unusual in that it is one of the few isolated offshore reefs in the Rabaul area. Just 6km west of the Kulau Beach Resort, it is a long narrow reef with deep water off its northern end. The reef here is exposed at low tide, so navigate carefully to prevent reef and boat damage.

The best diving is at either end of the reef and along the western side, where a near vertical wall has plenty of soft coral growth. This is a healthy and vibrant

Location: 6km (4 miles) west of Kulau Lodge

Depth Range: 0-40m (0-130ft) plus

Access: Boat

Expertise Rating: Intermediate

reef with many different corals and fish. It is one of the best reefs that can be

dived from Rabaul. Not only is the reef in excellent condition, it is easily reached, mostly sheltered and typically has excellent visibility. Slight currents run in the area.

Celestial nudibranch

80 Fringing Reefs

West of Midway Reef, the fringing reef along the northern shore becomes well developed. Diving from shore is possible once you've consulted with locals.

Liguan Reef Garden off Cape Liguan is one of the best, with excellent corals down to 30m and regular sightings of eagle rays, grey reef sharks and turtles.

Nearby, **Wanagamata Reef** is an easy dive accessible by boat or shore. Coral heads are scattered over the sandy bottom. Although larger fish are not common, all the usual reef fish appear

Location: Along shore east of Talili

Depth Range: 0-30m (0-100ft)

Access: Boat or Shore

Expertise Rating: Novice

in good numbers. This is a particularly good site for divers wishing to photograph anemonefish, butterflyfish and other reef dwellers.

81 Bangkok Pass

Some exceptional dive sites between Rabaul and Walindi can only be conveniently dived by live-aboard. In particular the region around Cape Lambert, 75km west of Rabaul, has some exceptional reef passes through a large barrier reef, and a maze of interesting islands and reefs inside a lagoon formed by the barrier reef.

Location: Southwest of Cape Lambert

Depth Range: 5-40m (16-130ft) plus

Access: Live-aboard

Expertise Rating: Advanced

One of the best dives is Bangkok Pass on the outer barrier southwest of Cape Lambert. This is a wide pass with optimum conditions when a slight current flows into the lagoon from the west. Visibility is usually 30m or better but is reduced if the current flows the other way. Either side of the pass may be dived; however, the northern side is often better.

Eagle rays, massive dogtooth tuna and Spanish mackerel, grey reef and silvertip sharks visit the area, but scalloped hammerheads—in groups of up to a dozen—are the star attraction.

Other reef passes in the area produce excellent action although the reef formations are not as good as in areas such as Kimbe Bay. Currents can be a problem as they are sometimes quite fierce. Diving is always much better when the current is flowing into the lagoon.

Visibility inside the lagoon depends significantly on local rainfall but since the reefs are filled with plenty of small creatures suitable for macrophotography, this is not a critical consideration. Much exploration still has to be done in this area.

82 Baldwin's Bridge

At Cape St. George there is an unnamed rock island sticking up from a small reef offshore on the eastern side of the Cape. Around the southeast side of the reef a huge natural arch reaches across from the main reef to a second reef. At 27m you can swim under the arch, but beware—the bottom is at least 60m deep.

Location: Southern tip of New Ireland

Depth Range: 0-40m (0-130ft) plus

Access: Live-aboard

Expertise Rating: Advanced

The arch, known as Baldwin's Bridge, is covered with pink soft corals, sea whips and hydroids. Masses of fish swim around it and a population of grey reef sharks patrols back and forth under the bridge. It is a truly amazing sight, particularly in the typically crystal clear water.

The site is extremely difficult to dive most of the year as it is exposed to southeast swells and wind, and often has a strong current running through. The only time to attempt this dive is during the northwest season, and even then some luck is required.

BOB HALSTEAD

Baldwin's Bridge, a dramatic natural archway.

Kavieng Dive Sites

Divers are some of the most frequent visitors to this odd-shaped area of New Guinea. Kavieng has a world-wide reputation as one of the premiere places to observe wild pelagics.

Kavieng is steeped in history and is a scenic, tropical isle safe from the cyclone belt. The island of New Ireland is the shape of a giant rib, 360km (224 miles) long but not even 10km (6 miles) wide in several places. Don't let this odd geography fool you. Once there, you will find it mountainous; in some places the rugged hills fall straight into the sea.

Kavieng is small, but it does have a golf course, an eye-catching harbor and some tiny islets that are great day snorkels and picnicking sites. Local people are quite friendly and curious. Chats around the night fire are a great way to make new friends and learn something about how real Papua New Guineans live.

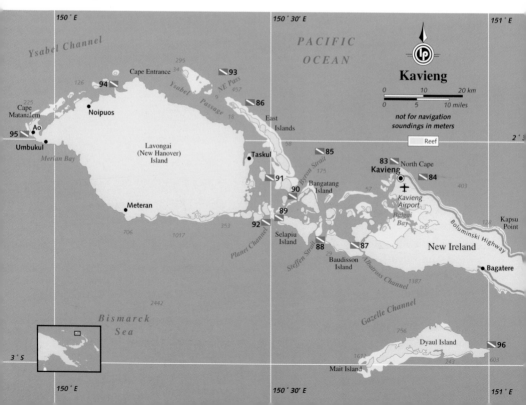

Kavieng Diving

Blessed with reefs swept with oceanic and tidal currents, Kavieng is the pelagic capital of the country. It is famous for its huge schools of barracuda and trevally, regular sightings of giant Queensland grouper and silvertip sharks. At Valerie's Reef, divers can experience close-up encounters with these magnificent sharks, which come to feed in the area.

New Ireland curves away to the northwest from Cape St. George. Off the northwestern end of New Ireland is New Hanover. Between the two islands is a maze of reefs, coral islands, mangroves and passes—a marine nursery of amazing fertility. The west coast, bordering the Bismark Sea, features a coral wall, with the narrow fringing reefs suddenly dropping to over 1,000m (3,280ft). The northern and northeastern coasts have a gradually sloping seabed and a more extensive system of offshore reefs.

Although Kavieng waters have many sheltered coral gardens suitable for all levels of divers, those wishing to experience the big action dives should be prepared to cope with sometimes difficult conditions. Certainly experience with currents is a great help.

Kavieng Dive Sites

	Good Snorkeling	Novice	Intermediate	Advanced
83 Echuca Patch & the *Der Yang*				●
84 Kaplaman Reef			●	
85 Turtle Reef		●	●	
86 Valerie's Reef				●
87 Albatross Pass & B25 Aircraft Wreck				●
88 Steffen Strait				●
89 Byron Strait				●
90 Nub Island			●	
91 Kate Aircraft Wreck		●		
92 Planet Channel				●
93 Big Fish Reef				●
94 Three Islands Harbour	●	●		
95 Ao Island				●
96 Dyaul Point	●	●		

83 Echuca Patch & the *Der Yang*

Just 2km from the eastern entrance to Kavieng Harbour, Echuca Patch is a magnificent and convenient dive site. The sausage-shaped reef rises from a white sand bottom at 50m to a peak 15m below the surface at its southern end. The reef slopes off at the sides and gradually descends along its length to 30m at its northern end, where the scuttled wreck of the *Der Yang* fishing boat rests.

Location: Eastern entrance to Kavieng Harbour

Depth Range: 15-30m (50-100ft) plus

Access: Boat

Expertise Rating: Advanced

A diver explores the wreck of the *Der Yang*.

The reeftop and sides are covered with hard corals, many sea fans and whips. The peak of the reef has splendid growths of a yellow soft coral. The water is usually very clear with at least 40m visibility. The dive can be tricky if there are ocean swells or if a current is running. Nevertheless, this is a "must-see" dive, not only for the marvelous scenery and photogenic wreck, but also the likely event of bumping into one or more giant Queensland groupers living on the wreck.

Schooling barracuda circle above the wreck when the current is from the northeast, while trevally, eagle rays and dogtooth tuna parade around the reef. On the reeftop among the branching corals, you'll encounter several large schools of two-spot snapper. At least two dives are necessary to explore this reef comfortably.

84 Kaplaman Reef

East of North Cape and only a 15–minute fast boat ride from Kavieng are a series of offshore reefs. Kaplaman Reef is off Kaplaman village and an interesting dive site that undulates (in a rather confusing manner) over a large area. The best plan for diving it is to find the shallow part of the reef—at about 8m—on the side

Location: East of North Cape

Depth Range: 8-40m (26-130ft) plus

Access: Boat

Expertise Rating: Intermediate

receiving any current (typically from the east), then work your way down the slopes into the current. There are excellent hard corals but also large sponges, occasional sea fans and gorgonians, particularly in deeper water. You'll see fine schooling fish life, possible sharks and giant groupers.

85 Turtle Reef

Turtle Reef rises from 200m to patches only 8m deep. The reef is far too large to explore on a single dive and is rather confusing to dive since there is no defined drop-off and many ridges, hills and fingers. The scenery is spectacular with wide expanses of perfect hard coral growth, patches of pink and yellow soft corals around the larger bommies and gorgonians deeper down the reef slopes.

Location: 7km (4 miles) north of Bangatang Island

Depth Range: 8-40m (26-130ft) plus

Access: Boat

Expertise Rating: Intermediate

The water is usually very clear, but visibility can be reduced if currents are flowing out of the lagoon through Byron Strait. The swirling of the currents on the surface above the reef leads villagers to avoid it. The fishing is not good and the large fish schools so common on other, nearby reefs are strangely lacking here.

The absence of fishermen has enabled divers to befriend several hawksbill turtles. The turtles are easily tamed; they are so used to divers that they will approach closely without any fear. It is not uncommon to have one or two turtles follow you around for the whole dive. Even snorkelers can interact with the turtles when they come to the surface to breathe. Avoid taking advantage of this trust and grabbing, touching or feeding the turtles.

BOB HALSTEAD

Hawksbill turtles are curious and trusting of divers. Be respectful of the turtle and its environment, and you'll have a friend for life.

86 | Valerie's Reef

On the northeast side of New Hanover Island is a chain of uncharted reefs mostly rising from the sloping bottom in to 10m or so from the surface. For many years these reefs have been a feeding station for a family of silvertip sharks.

Divers started feeding the sharks in 1989 when the unique nature of the site was realized. The site is dominated by silvertip sharks but lacks grey reef sharks, who frenzy when fed. Silvertips are far more controlled and generally approach the baits in turn. The sharks are now so relaxed with divers that it is no longer necessary to use baits to bring them close.

The site was named after Valerie Taylor, an Australian underwater photographer who has worked with sharks all her life. Divers can enjoy the close company of up to nine of these magnificent beasts that remain much misunderstood by most non-divers.

Bull sharks and blacktip sharks occasionally visit the area, but never a

Location: Northeast New Hanover Island

Depth Range: 10-40m (35-130ft) plus

Access: Boat

Expertise Rating: Advanced

grey reef shark. Valerie's Reef sharks have now achieved worldwide acclaim and are an incredibly valuable resource for PNG.

Fortunately the local villagers realize the value of these sharks for tourism, and anyone contemplating shark finning in the area would have to face the wrath of the villagers who own local fishing rights, but prefer to keep the sharks alive. Of course, not only are the sharks a great attraction for tourist divers, they also help keep the reefs healthy by culling sick and injured fish, a vital consideration for the local fishermen.

BOB HALSTEAD

Silvertip sharks generally live in deeper inshore waters along drop-offs and banks.
They feed at any depth, eating everything from rays and octopus, to mid-range and surface fish.

Feeding the Frenzy

A shark feed can be both exhilarating and educational—the ultimate illustrated lecture. But there are downsides to these staged performances:

Danger: Several guides and at least one tourist have been bitten, according to the International Shark Attack File, and as the number of organized shark feeds increases, so too does the potential for further injuries.

Unnatural Acts: Feeding the same territorial animals time and again may condition sharks to lose their wariness of humans (and vice versa). Sharks that grow dependent on "free lunches" may unlearn vital survival skills. Some have developed dangerous Pavlovian responses to the sound of revving boat motors.

Reef Damage: Sometimes a dozen or more divers are dropped on a feeding station at once, often in shifts. No experience beyond an open water certification is generally required, compounding the potential for site destruction.

Divers curious about shark behavior have numerous options for natural open water encounters, experiences far more natural and spontaneous than trained fish circuses.

—Larry Clinton

87 Albatross Pass & B25 Aircraft Wreck

The south coast near Kavieng is easily accessible through the twisting man-grove-lined channels formed by the main island and countless smaller islands. Albatross Channel is the most easterly and provides clear passage for small ships.

Albatross Pass is a wonderful dive site where the channel meets the Bismark Sea. The site falls away vertically, from 8m to a sand ledge at 30m, before finally dropping into the abyss. The wall is nicely sculptured with crevices, ridges and excellent growths of black corals and gorgonians. Schools of bigeye trevally, barracuda, batfish and many smaller species parade up and down the edge of the wall, but it is the shark population that will impress more than anything.

Location: South coast New Ireland near Kavieng

Depth Range: 8-40m (26-130ft) plus

Access: Boat

Expertise Rating: Advanced

It is possible to drop to the sand ledge and photograph upward toward the wall, with sharks silhouetted against the blue surface. Giant groupers are often seen and this is one of the few areas in northern PNG where manta rays occur, particularly the small *mobula* species.

This dive should only be made with an incoming current. Not only does this make the visibility a lot better—up to 40m—but this is also when schooling fish and shark action is at its best. The Port Moresby tide tables will give you a rough approximation of the incoming tide, which seems to coincide well with

BOB HALSTEAD

Grey reef sharks seem to like strong currents.

high tide in Port Moresby. This rule can also be used for the other channels on the south coast near Kavieng. Between Albatross Pass and Lessening Island lies the almost intact wreck of a wartime B25 Bomber, shot down in 1944. This dive is called **Stubborn Hellion** and is shallow, resting in only 12m.

88 Steffen Strait

Steffen Strait is the main shipping channel into Kavieng and exciting diving is possible on any of several patch reefs just outside the entrance to the strait. The best is probably **Peter's Patch**, about 1km due south of the eastern entrance to the strait.

A current often runs over this reef, which is formed like a ridge that narrows as it descends to the east. The ridge slopes in places but also bottoms out vertically in some spots.

The best dive is with the current coming from the east and flowing into the strait. As you descend the ridge, you'll encounter increasing numbers of fish

Location: Southern entrance to Steffen Strait

Depth Range: 8-40m (26-130ft) plus

Access: Boat

Expertise Rating: Advanced

and sharks. The reef here is excellent with a mixture of plate corals on top and sea fans and whips on the slopes. A marlin has been seen swimming off the ridge and two golden cowries were found on one memorable dive.

The current running over Peter's Patch means hardy marine life and lots of action.

BOB HALSTEAD

89 Byron Strait

The next passage to the west is Byron Strait, where you'll find excellent wall diving on either side of the entrance. A couple of coral towers connected by a ridge make for very good diving if the current is flowing out of the strait.

Nautilus Ridge is a finger of reef projecting on the eastern side of the entrance. This proves to be a very productive spot for setting a nautilus trap. This technique involves a special trap, set overnight in 250-300m. In the morning, trapped nautilus are brought to the surface, and then immediately taken down the drop-off and released. This is not harmful to the nautilus and allows divers to study and photograph these fascinating creatures before they swim back down to their deep homes.

Location: Southern entrance to Byron Strait

Depth Range: 9-27m (30-90ft) plus

Access: Boat

Expertise Rating: Advanced

Nautilus Ridge is rather barren on top in 5m, as are many of the reefs in the area; however, down the wall the situation quickly changes with good coral and gorgonian growth and plenty of fish life.

Byron Wall at the southwest entrance to Byron Strait is a beautiful wall with deep crevices and even a swim-through near the corner. You can dive the wall

Nautilus generally live in waters 60-750m deep.

A rare Randall's anthias appears in Byron's Strait.

Valerie Taylor watches as a nautilus falls back to its deep home after being released from the trap.

over the front edge but also around into the start of the strait. Black coral trees and sponges are common as are lone sharks, including hammerheads. One of the fascinating aspects of this site for fish photographers is the abundance of the more unusual basslets. These exquisite little fish can be found all down the wall and include the bicolor, Randall's and Cooper's varieties.

Byron Wall must be dived on an incoming tide. If the current is flowing out, **Judy's Reef**, a coral tower 900m or

so to the northwest, is an excellent dive site. It misses the river of murky water that pours out from the lagoon. This small reef has a flat top at 5m, a wall around most of its circumference and a dramatic ledge at 30m off its western tip. Large sharks are often seen here and the ledge is beautifully decorated with black coral whips and gorgonians. The wall is undercut in places and there is a swim-through on the southern side at 22m, the western entrance to which is almost entirely obstructed by a sea fan.

90 Nub Island

If strong winds make diving the south coast uncomfortable, it is possible to make a pleasant drift dive beside Nub Island. Here the reef slope has rich growths of gorgonians and sponges to 22m and is visited by many reef fish. This is low risk and easy drift diving since the water is always flat calm and the top of the reef less than a meter deep.

A boat cruising past Nub Island into the lagoon and towards the tiny Moritz

Location: Byron Strait

Depth Range: 0-22m (0-72ft)

Access: Boat

Expertise Rating: Intermediate

Rock off of Patio Island, will pass over a small patch reef known as **Mala-canthus Patch**. Named for its healthy population of tilefish (*Malacanthus lato-vittatus*), this reef is a perfect place to stop for the night. After anchoring in sand on the edge of the patch, divers can explore the scruffy coral for all sorts

Bugs for Dinner

The painted reef lobster, *Panulirus versicolor*, is found in small numbers throughout PNG. Reef lobster fisheries, such as the one in New Hanover, generally take rock lobster, *Panulirus pencillatus*, which lives in very shallow water in the surf zone and is rarely seen by divers not actively looking for it.

Dive boats typically stock up with live lobsters by buying them from villagers. Coconut crab is also a special delicacy available in some of the islands. Visitors are reminded that it is illegal for non-residents to remove any living organism from the PNG seabed without authority.

Spanish dancer nudibranch

of treasures. Look for Spanish dancers, pleurobranchs and other nudibranchs, live shells—including map cowries and the highly venomous geography cones—stonefish, scorpionfish, and spiny lobsters.

The reef rises from sand at 20m to 8m. Although the coral is not all that splendid, there are some colorful soft corals and sea fans. A current sometimes runs over the reef, which you should check before diving.

91 Kate Aircraft Wreck

In the lagoon close to Anelaua Island is the wreck of a Japanese "Kate" three-seater dive bomber. The wreck lies upright in the narrow passage between the southern tip of the island and a reef to its west, not far from a stone jetty. The

Location: Anelaua Island

Depth: 10m (33ft)

Access: Boat

Expertise Rating: Novice

wreck depth is only 10m but, unfortunately, the water is seldom very clear.

On one occasion the water suddenly cleared and it was possible to take beautiful photographs of this interesting aircraft that is still intact with its its propeller in place. Although good visiblity is rare, the site is always sheltered.

92 Planet Channel

Sailing south from Anelaua Island, small ships can make clear passage through Planet Channel back to the south coast to one of the most fantastic areas for diving near Kavieng. Several different dives are possible in this area.

The easiest is probably the drift dive through Planet Channel. It is best on an incoming tide when swift currents flow through the 3km-long channel. The western side slopes steeply and is awash at the surface but descends to about 22m.

Sea fans, giant sponges, sea whips and soft corals thrive on the slope. The vari-

Location: South of Anelaua island

Depth Range: 0-40m (0-130ft) plus

Access: Boat

Expertise Rating: Advanced

ous coral ledges and bommies are home to many reef fish. It is possible to get out of the current in the shallows. Or you can get out down the slope nearer the center of the channel to experience its full force and race effortlessly along the bottom.

BOB HALSTEAD

A narrow ridge of reef extends over the passage, where it widens as it meets the ocean. The southwest end of the ridge is separated from the fringing reef by a canyon called **Eagle Ray Pass**. Both sides of the pass, which are usually within site of each other, are vertical and undercut. Between them is a lip of coral rubble and sand at about 35m, which then drops away steeply.

On an incoming tide a school of up to 30 eagle rays sometimes hovers in the entrance. The top of the ridge is only at 5m at this end and dives may be made in the pass or over the front drop-off. The incoming tide can be fierce but you can find shelter inside the pass. The tide effect is minimal down the front face at 10m or so.

This is a stunning site offering some fantastic diving. Remember, it can be tricky since the current can change rapidly. It is often a struggle to get to the start of the wall at 20m. Divers have been caught by the change of tide and have found themselves drifting out to sea. It is essential that a good lookout stays on the boat while divers are in the water and that divers carry safety sausages or other signaling devices. Excellent dives are possible along the whole length of the ridge, which extends for about 400m from Eagle Ray Pass to the fringing reef on the eastern side of Planet Channel.

93 Big Fish Reef

An exceptional reef, 4km on the seaward side of Northeast Pass off New Hanover Island, rises to a plateau at 12m with ridges extending from its corners. Rather too large to comfortably circumnavigate on a single dive, the best plan with this reef is to carefully note any current flowing—typically from the southeast—and go straight to the ridge nearest that side of the reef.

Location: Northeast of New Hanover Island

Depth Range: 12-40m (40-130ft) plus

Access: Live-aboard

Expertise Rating: Advanced

BOB HALSTEAD

Here you will find the phenomenon that gave this site the name Big Fish Reef. Great clouds of barracuda, trevally and batfish wheel around the masses of reef fish. Eagle rays are common. Some good hard coral grows down the slopes, though the reeftop is patchy. Orange sponges, sea whips and soft corals grow on the bottom of the slope. The sea bed at 50m is white sand and rubble.

Sharks, including bull sharks, have been seen here and during one memorable cruise a beautiful and friendly whale shark made its debut. The water is usually very clear and you can expect visibility better than 45m.

94 Three Islands Harbour

Three Islands Harbour, a snug and safe anchorage protected by three small islands, was used by Japanese forces during WWII. Some of the ships that were sunk during battle remain, including two small ships reported to be submarine chasers, near the shore.

Location: North coast of New Hanover Island

Depth Range: 0-22m (0-72ft)

Access: Live-aboard

Expertise Rating: Novice

The bow of one sticks out of the water, pointing upward at the edge of a reef. The rest of the ship sits in shallow water with its guns and other artifacts still largely intact. Beware the water clarity this close to shore is usually poor.

Close to Dunung Island, near one of the passages that leads into the harbor, lies a magnificent armed freighter wreck. Reported to be the *Sanko Maru*, the wreck rests on its starboard side in only 22m. It is smothered with soft corals, sea fans and other marine growth.

One safe way to penetrate the wreck is to swim up the inside of the huge funnel that is open at both ends. The wreck catches the tidal currents, which have created ideal conditions for the marine life that make this wreck so special.

Visibility is typically 15m but it is still a good macro dive, with many nudibranchs, flat worms, pipefish and other interesting critters. A large Queensland grouper often appears here and schooling fish—particularly trevally—abound. Boats should anchor in the sand beside the wreck, then tie a line to the port side near a large and complete crack in the hull. If you start at the crack then descend toward the stern (east), you'll see a pair of masts pointing out over the sand.

Ardeadoris egretta, one of PNG's many nudibranchs.

BOB HALSTEAD

The Mini-Submarine is now encrusted in corals.

Follow this direction and about 50m over the sand you'll come to a perfect wreck of a **Japanese Mini-Submarine** sitting upright in 22m. This submarine was caught alongside a ship when it was attacked by American bombers. When it became obvious that the ship was sinking, the submarine's three crewmembers scuttled it.

The twin counter-rotating propellers are intact at the stern and the periscope and torpedo tubes are easy to photograph. Fortunately for today's divers, the crew that salvaged the shipwreck (which has never been definitely identified) missed the submarine, probably as it cannot be seen from the main wreck.

95 Ao Island

Ao Island is near the western cape of New Hanover, Cape Matanalem. Just 300m from Ao is one of the most thrilling dives in all of PNG.

Chapman's Reef is not for the faint-hearted. A strong current often runs from the southeast and strikes the end of a long narrow ridge. A sudden drop-off tumbles to depths far too deep for scuba divers. Huge schools of barracuda, trevally, snappers, surgeonfish, batfish and fusiliers assemble at the edge of the drop. Sharks and giant groupers patrol the deeper water. Dogtooth tuna and Spanish mackerel flash through the clouds of fish. Eagle rays, whale sharks and other big fish visit here too. In the electric atmosphere of this dive, anything could swim by.

Various techniques make this dive possible. The easiest method is to simply anchor the boat on top of the relatively barren ridge near a deep crack that slices

Location: Western tip of New Hanover

Depth Range: 8-40m (26-130ft) plus

Access: Live-aboard

Expertise Rating: Advanced

the ridge and get a small boat to drop you off up-current of the wall. Strangely, the current has been observed to be strongest on neap tides.

There is a second reef called **Chapman's #2** to the southeast, separated from the Ao Island fringing reef by a channel. This is also a first-rate dive and is usually a little easier than Chapman's Reef. There is a wall on the eastern side and a ridge ending in a bommie on the northwest corner. Both places are liable to produce eagle rays sightings. This reef is shallower on top with depths of about 5m and sea fans and soft corals are found along the sides of the reef.

A little farther along the coast to the southeast directly off Taun Village is another reef isolated from the fringing reef by a channel. This one is narrow enough that divers can easily cross it to dive the wall of the fringing reef. However, the best diving is at the northeast end, where there is a steep drop-off and a wealth of fish life. There are many scenic views on this reef with different coral formations ideal for wide-angle photography.

A diver swims with schooling barracuda at Chapman's Reef.

96 Dyaul Point

On the northern side of the tip at Dyaul Point is a steep drop-off that shelves at about 18m, forming a small lagoon with the fringing reef. There are three coral towers rising at the edge of the drop-off.

The easterly tower, in 5m, is relatively barren, but the other two and the lagoon have fabulous corals of all varieties and excellent fish life. This is an easy and relaxing dive. The water here is usually very clear and constantly fed by a slight current.

Location: Southeast tip of Dyaul Island

Depth Range: 0-40m (0-130ft) plus

Access: Live-aboard

Expertise Rating: Novice

An Islander launches off Egum Atoll.

PNG is blessed with myriad small, remote islands, many of which have exciting, lush reefs promising wonderful diving. These sites are becoming more accessible as the live-aboard dive fleet cruises these areas. Exploratory diving is often a major part of the itinerary and, for those interested in being among the first to ever explore a particular site, this is quite a thrill.

Some of these islands are inhabited by just a small family or clan, while others support a larger population. Still, the lifestyles of island residents are undoubtedly subsistence living. Arrangements to dive in these isles must be made before you can jump in the water. The boat captain will go ashore, perhaps with a mate, and explain the intentions of the divers. The captain will also make arrangements to buy fresh fruits and vegetables, which helps the local economy and puts variety on the live-aboard dinner table.

As you visit these islands, you can see how people truly survive off the land and sea. Islanders use the fertile, volcanic soils to grow foods and tobacco. The strong smell of coconut oil permeates the villages and the coconut tree provides food,

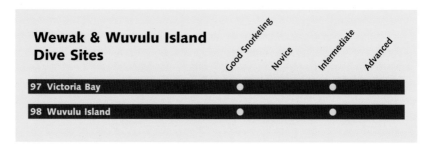

Wewak & Wuvulu Island Dive Sites	Good Snorkeling	Novice	Intermediate	Advanced
97 Victoria Bay	●		●	
98 Wuvulu Island	●		●	

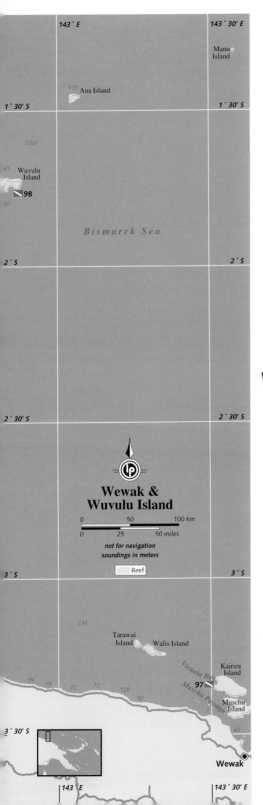

shelter and copra for cash. It is the lifeblood of the islanders, who are some of the last people on earth to live this way.

Simple, efficient homes are the norm. Some are quite elaborate with raised floors, rooms and porches. Others are not much more than lean-tos.

Some islanders work the land and have little dependence on the sea. Some have small outriggers, used only to traverse the inner lagoons. Others are quite accomplished fishermen and may even have "power canoes,"—Yamaha hulls with gas or diesel engines. The children of the villages regard divers with great interest and may paddle out in small outriggers to follow your bubbles. Some of the famous photographic silhouettes of the South Pacific come from these isolated islands.

Wewak & Wuvulu Island

BOB HALSTEAD
Friendly villagers in Victoria Bay.

The town of Wewak is a gateway to the Sepik River, which is famous for the villages along its banks and waterways. Sepik villagers have distinctive traditional houses, which you can see re-created in the National Parliament building in Port Moresby. The villagers are also prolific carvers and the sales to tourists provide a vital part of the area's income.

97 Victoria Bay

Kairuru Island off Wewak town in Victoria Bay has excellent diving on two Japanese WWII wrecks. The identity of the Victoria Bay wrecks is uncertain but some people believe that the largest could be the *India Maru*. It has been the subject of intensive searches by salvage divers seeking the gold bullion that the ship carried as cargo. If the wreck is indeed the *India Maru*, the gold has long since disappeared.

The upright, armed freighter sits on sand at 37m and is about 90m long. The

Location: Western side of Kairuru Island

Depth Range: 0-37m (0-120ft)

Access: Boat

Expertise Rating: Intermediate

BOB HALSTEAD

Blue-ringed angelfish on the *India Maru*.

deck is at 25m and although most of the superstructure was bombed, there are massive trees of black coral and prolific fish life, making it very attractive for wide-angle photography.

Victoria Bay shelters the wreck from the southeast trade winds and currents tend to be mild. The second wreck is in 18m without its stern, which remains to be found. The bow section is about 25m long and is also photogenic, with its port anchor hanging from the hausepipe and just touching the sand.

98 Wuvulu Island

Jean Michael Cousteau, who conducted several Project Ocean Search expeditions to Wuvulu, made the island famous in the 1970s. Its pristine environment and rave reviews from visiting divers inspired the construction of a diver's lodge.

The logistics of getting to this remote spot in small aircraft doomed the commercial success of the project. The Wuvulu Lodge still stands on the beach but is seldom used. Perhaps someday the lodge will be reopened so that divers can explore the coral walls that drop just a few meters off the beach.

These sites are weather dependent and there is no anchorage anywhere for ves-

Location: 200km northwest of Wewak

Depth Range: 0-40m (0-130ft) plus

Access: Shore

Expertise Rating: Intermediate

sels larger than a dinghy. The reef wall has many swim-throughs and one deep cave with stalactites. There are many turtles, and reef fish are plentiful in the clear waters.

TIM ROCK

Hermit & Ninigo Islands

The Hermit and Ninigo island groups are about 240km (149 miles) to the north/northeast of Wewak. With latitude of just over one degree south of the equator, these islands offer a great variety of dive sites and sheltered anchorages. Both groups are inhabited and the villagers are very friendly.

The only negative side to these islands is that, through live fish exports, the villagers have played a part in the exploitation of their own fishing resources. Divers accustomed to the abundance of most PNG reefs will notice the scarcity of large reef fish here.

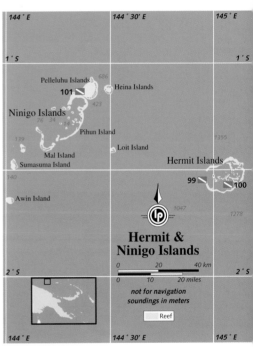

Hermit &
Ninigo Islands

0   20   40 km
0   10   20 miles
*not for navigation
soundings in meters*

Reef

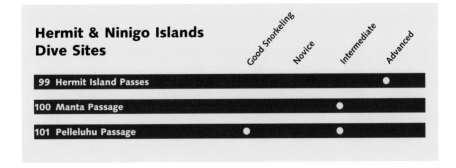

Hermit & Ninigo Islands Dive Sites	Good Snorkeling	Novice	Intermediate	Advanced
99 Hermit Island Passes				●
100 Manta Passage			●	
101 Pelleluhu Passage		●	●	

99 Hermit Island Passes

The Hermit Islands atoll has two main passages through the outer barrier reef to the northwest and west, and a smaller passage to the southeast. The northwest entrance has very good diving on its southwest side, inside the lagoon where soft corals and sea fans abound. Here, contrary to the usual expectations, an outgoing current will produce the best diving as masses of fish congregate to feed on the plankton-rich waters of the lagoon.

Location: Northwest, West and Southeast lagoon entrances

Depth Range: 5-40m (16-130ft) plus

Access: Boat

Expertise Rating: Advanced

The visibility may not be the best but you can expect at least 15m and the site is always sheltered. On the outside, the corals are not in the best condition, but the diving is good, particularly if manta rays and sharks are hanging around.

The west entrance has better diving with clear water on the outside wall, near a wreck that can be seen from the reeftop to the south. The wall here is adorned with sea fans and whips at 18 to 30m.

The southeast entrance can experience large ocean swells from the southeast. When it is calm, divers will discover that there are actually two passages with a reef between them.

In 1995, coral deterioration was reported in this area, the cause of which was not obvious. Plenty of fish can still be found and a pod of friendly dolphins in the passes sometimes swims with divers.

North of this entrance is **Alacrity Harbour**, accessible only from the ocean. There is very good diving on the northern finger of reef securing the harbor. It is possible to anchor a small boat on the outer tip of the finger in 3m of water and descend the steep wall. Expect to be greeted by silvertip and grey reef sharks.

Spinner dolphins occasionally greet divers at the entrance to the lagoon.

100 | Manta Passage

The lagoon inside the barrier reef has several large islands, one of which had a castle built on it by trader and plantation owner Rudolph Whalen around the early 1900s. Only the foundations now remain. The building was demolished by a plantation manager who was tired of walking up the hill every day. He used the leftover material to build a more modest house on the beach. Deer introduced to the islands by Rudolph Whalen still thrive.

Between Akib and Luf islands is Manta Passage, 22m deep and bounded by fringing reefs. Isolated coral bommies break up the otherwise uniform sand and rubble bottom.

Location: Between Akib and Luf Islands

Depth: 22m (72ft)

Access: Boat

Expertise Rating: Intermediate

This passage is well worth diving due to the likelihood of seeing manta rays. The rays are not always present and the visibility is not always good, but with a bit of luck and careful diving superb manta experiences are possible. On no account should divers attempt to touch the mantas, as they will disappear.

BOB HALSTEAD

101 Pelleluhu Passage

The Ninigo Islands harbor three large lagoons, two of which may be entered for secure anchorage. The dive not to be missed in this group is Pelleluhu Passage.

This passage falls to deep ocean water at each end, which guarantees excellent visibility, the possibility of seeing large pelagics and plenty of sharks. Set up a drift dive and drift along the passage walls with the prevailing current. Since the passage is about 4km long, there is plenty to see.

For those who prefer to dive from an anchored boat, there is an anchorage spot on the southern side of the passage, near the western entrance where a spur of reef stands out from the wall. Boats can anchor in 8m and dive the

Location: Between Pelleluhu and main Ninigo lagoon

Depth Range: 8-40m (26-130ft) plus

Access: Boat

Expertise Rating: Intermediate

spur. Masses of fish congregate here possibly because, no matter which way the current is flowing through the main channel, an eddy causes it to constantly flow from the east.

You'll see many coral trout and eagle rays, in addition to all the usual pelagic and reef fish. Once a tiger shark was seen attacking and eating one of the plentiful turtles that frequent the passage. A huge pod of a thousand or more spinner dolphins is resident in the passage, which is sheltered in most weather conditions.

To the south of the Ninigo Lagoon are four reef passes into the lagoon that also have excellent diving. You can anchor inside the reef then dive the passes using a dinghy. Incoming tides are better and the water is astonishingly clear. Although the currents can be strong, eagle rays like to hover and luxuriant growths of sea fans and black corals thrive. Sharks are also common.

Southwest of the Ninigo Islands, Sumasuma offers a sheltered anchorage in the southeast season with excellent diving on two nearby spurs of reef. The eastern tip is best for pelagics and the western for macro subjects.

BOB HALSTEAD
A grey reef shark swims among schooling fish.

Egum Atoll

Egum, in Milne Bay Province, is a classic atoll with a circular lagoon about 33km (21 miles) across. Several islands dot the rim and center of the lagoon, where you'll find the best anchorage.

People are friendly and participate in the traditional Kula Ring, which encompasses islands in the Solomon Sea. Once a year, a trader and his delegation travel in elaborately decorated canoes to the islands in the Kula Ring. Gifts are exchanged, thereby creating lasting bonds between clans. Traditionally, the exchange involved families of high status, helping to reinforce clan-based hierarchies.

BOB HALSTEAD

Apart from being astonishingly seaworthy, traditional canoes are works of art.

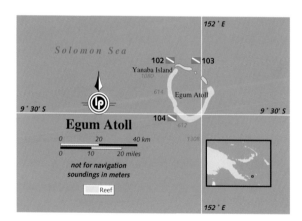

Egum Atoll Dive Sites

	Good Snorkeling	Novice	Intermediate	Advanced
102 Northwest Pass			●	
103 Egum Rock				●
104 Hollis Reef			●	

102 Northwest Pass

The Northwest Pass on an incoming tide is a great dive. Boats can anchor in the pass right on the edge of a vertical drop-off. Expect to see large numbers of big fish, including giant grouper and hammerhead sharks. The reef is not much to speak of but the fish life, when the tide is right, is exceptional. The dive is a waste of time with an outgoing current, as the fish disappear, along with the visibility.

Location: Northwest entrance to the lagoon

Depth Range: 3-40m (10-130ft) plus

Access: Boat

Expertise Rating: Intermediate

103 Egum Rock

Egum Rock rises from over 600m-deep water. The sheer-sided rock has sparse shrubs growing on it and is inhabited by thousands of sea birds—the smell is dreadful.

The water surrounding the rock has a narrow shelf to about 10m, where it drops. This is a wonderful dive where large pelagics and sharks, schools of barracuda and trevally, and masses of tropical reef fish swarm. The yellow and

Location: North of Yanaba Island

Depth Range: 5-40m (16-130ft) plus

Access: Boat

Expertise Rating: Advanced

Bigeye trevally swarm through the passes at Egum Rock.

silver pyramid butterflyfish is present in huge numbers on the reef slopes and dense schools of the rarer red pinjalo snapper are always around.

Currents sometimes make diving here uncomfortable. It is possible to drift around each side of the rock however, and the currents are mostly modest. In still conditions divers can circumnavigate the rock comfortably in about 30 minutes. Visibility is consistently excellent. Keep an eye open out into the blue as schooling hammerheads are known to cruise by.

A school of red pinjalo snapper.

104 Hollis Reef

An unusual dive outside the lagoon is Hollis Reef, a patch reef accessible only in calm weather with a depth of about 5m on top. On the southeast side hundreds of large horizontal pink sea fans adorn the near-vertical wall. They are horizontal because the ocean swells normally reaching this reef, cause vertical currents up and down the reef face. Expect to encounter abundant pelagics and reef fish at this site.

Location: Outside lagoon on southwest corner

Depth Range: 5-40m (16-130ft) plus

Access: Boat

Expertise Rating: Intermediate

Horizontal sea fans at Hollis Reef.

Crown, Long & Bagabag Islands

TIM ROCK
A Long Islander cooks bananas over an open fire.

The trip to Crown Island on a good day takes about eight hours from Madang. The majestic volcanic peaks of Long Island first appear on the horizon followed by Crown's lone crater.

Sparsely inhabited with only one family living on its northern slopes, Long Island has an inland freshwater lake. But the jungle is thick and grows right to the shoreline with towering trees sprouting up from the interior. This makes shoreline exploration fun but penetration of the jungle tough going.

Long is an intriguing isle with a superb caldera and two active, usually cloud-shrouded volcanoes. It has black sand beaches and incredible sunsets can be seen along the west side. There are three small villages at the west end and another series of villages to the southeast. The lighthouse is the only real sign of modern

Crown, Long & Bagabag Islands Dive Sites	Good Snorkeling	Novice	Intermediate	Advanced
105 Batfish Lagoon	●	●		
106 The Saddles	●			●
107 Crown Corner				●
108 Hawkfish & Julien's Reefs				●
109 East Slope	●	●		
110 Village Log	●	●		
111 Mad Dog Reef				●
112 Bagabag Bay	●	●		
113 Bagabag Wall				●
114 Barracuda Seamount				●
115 Western Drop-Off				●

civilization, along with a small landing strip. The diving here is close to the island and many sites are good for multiple dives.

Friendly families willing to sell produce and other tasty treats live in well-kept compounds on Bagabag. This island has steep rising hills and beautifully secluded bays. Small copra plantations give the jungle some semblance of order along the slopes leading up from the sandy shores. All the trappings of a PNG holiday are found here: deep blue water, coconut tree-lined shores and kids in wooden outriggers frolicking in the sea. It has some great snorkeling spots and also some incredible pelagic and drift diving.

TIM ROCK

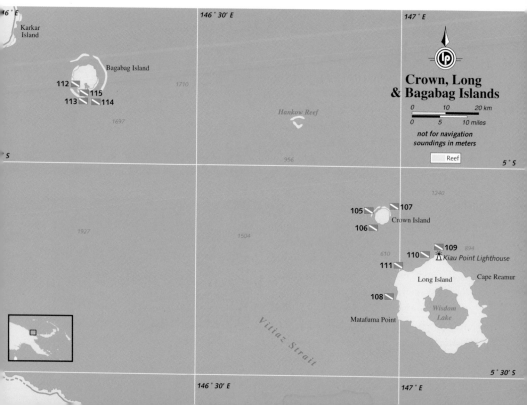

105 Batfish Lagoon

This protected deep inner lagoon (50m near the barrier reef) has some fine shallow dives, large coral bommies and muck diving in a large sandy bay. There is a large school of garden eels at 10m. Mantis shrimp, spinecheek clownfish, schooling juvenile batfish and lots of small critters abound here.

Night diving is good, with plentiful fan coral crabs and large hermit crabs. Unusual sand anemones and sea pens poke up from the sea floor at night. Large

Location: Western side, Crown

Depth Range: 6-25m (20-82ft)

Access: Boat

Expertise Rating: Novice

turtles have been spotted more than once. Currents are negligible in here. Snorkelers will enjoy the shallows at high tide.

Muck divers keep an eye out for mantis shrimp.

A sand anemone grows on the sandy floor.

106 The Saddles

A series of barrier reefs on the west side of Crown Island lead from one surprise to the next. They run for about three miles and are home to large dogtooth tuna, eagle rays, solo and schooling grey reef and silvertip sharks. Immense hawksbill turtles, accompanied by remoras and a gathering of rainbow runners, make these large reptiles living ecosystems.

Barrel sponges, fans, soft corals and a wide, colorful variety of marine invertebrates can all be found along the outer wall. Large, motionless and well-camouflaged stonefish like the upper reef. The deep inner lagoon, with mostly rubble and patch reef inside, is home to many cuttlefish, nudibranchs and schooling

Location: Outer Barrier Reef, Crown

Depth Range: 6-40m (20-130ft) plus

Access: Boat

Expertise Rating: Advanced

A turtle swims back down after getting some air.

fusiliers. Spinner dolphins swim in this inner reef area.

These reefs have an incredible number of purple, orange and white ascidians.

Crown Pinnacle is another excellent site. Nearby, but distinctly separate from The Saddles, this lone pinnacle rises to

5m of the surface. The reef has immense giant tridacna clams in only 10m, including two sitting side-by-side.

Swarming fish, lots of anemones and invertebrate life are common here, including unusual nudibranchs and the ragged pipefish.

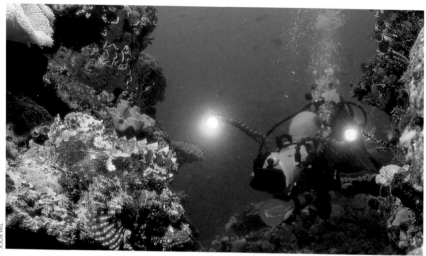

A videographer hones in on a large scorpionfish along the outer reef wall.

107 Crown Corner

At the northeast tip of Crown Island is a site called Crown Corner. A resident hammerhead shark, eagle rays, marbled reef rays and other big critters are com-

Location: Northeast Crown Island

Depth Range: 9-24m (30-80ft)

Access: Boat

Expertise Rating: Advanced

Schooling jacks gather to feed in the current.

mon here. A 6m current-scoured top drops to a sheer wall and is a good place to encounter schooling barracuda, bumphead parrotfish, Napoleon wrasse and a wall teeming with incredible fish life.

Currents can be tricky but also make for a great drift dive. Hang out at the tip and see what comes by.

108 Hawkfish & Julien's Reefs

Hawkfish Reef is great for spotting small life along the wall. A huge *Solencaulon* sea fan with snowy white polyps and a large hawkfish living in its branches punctuate the drop-off at 20m. Many varied nudibranchs, lots of corals and other marine invertebrates are found along protected crevices and pockets on the wall.

The usual abundance of fish and fusiliers are here and the site is loaded with sea anemones and various clownfish at the reeftop. The shallower reeftop is somewhat wave- and current-beaten.

Julien's Reef has superb big fish action with grey reefs, silvertips and a tiger shark or two. Big bumphead parrotfish, huge schools of rainbow runners and surgeonfish appear here along with the usual clouds of chromis. The swirling fish life is so busy here that a diver can actually get a

Location: Northwestern Long Island

Depth Range: 6-40m (20-130ft) plus

Access: Boat

Expertise Rating: Advanced

touch of vertigo from watching the constant movement.

A shallow western reef at 10 to 17m has giant tridacna clams, numerous anemones and multicolored crinoids with clingfish. The inner edge of the reef has a vertical wall with soft, amazingly colorful corals. Undercuts with various sea fans and large gorgonians on coral bommies thrive below the spectacular wall. This is superb, world-class diving.

A hawkfish rests near encrusting corals.

Soft coral and a giant clam.

109 East Slope

Diving in the volcanic sand of an old caldera produces some great surprises. Careful eyes will see various tiny shrimp, numerous nudibranchs, sand anemones and an interesting assortment of other invertebrate and juvenile fish life. Gobies and blind shrimp are in abundance. For those who like big things, visits from

Location: Northern Long Island

Depth Range: 5-33m (16-108ft)

Access: Boat

Expertise Rating: Novice

large sharks looking for crustaceans in the sand, and big sea turtles are on tap.

You can experience great night and dawn diving here. Night dives feature pleurobranchs, soft coral crabs and a host of flatworms, crabs and shrimps. A wall along the shore dips to 30m and has a vast array of tubastrea corals. Night dives are highlighted by visits from immense dogtooth tuna, sleeping turtles and even schooling jacks. On one dive, an eagle ray got confused in the lights and landed on a diver's head before soaring into the night.

Tiny shrimp gather at the foot of a crinoid.

110 Village Log

Near the small western village, marked by a log on the black sand beach, is an extreme drop-off. It drops quickly from 6 to 90m on a black sand slope. The reef near the northern point off the village is a

Location: Western Long Island

Depth Range: 5-40m (16-130ft) plus

Access: Boat

Expertise Rating: Novice

Look for this anemone and its fish at the point.

wall, bommie and sand dive all rolled into one. Cleaning stations have clouds of brilliant juvenile snappers and multitudes of anemones. A large collection of garden eels pick tidbits from the current-swept flats in front of the beach. Cuttlefish are also in abundance.

Undersea Light Shows

Cephalopods, such as squid and cuttlefish, are often seen on the Papuan reefs. Their amazing ability to change color and their rapid pulsing make them mesmerizing to watch.

Muck divers should be on the look out for flamboyant cuttlefish, living among debris on sandy slopes. In the same habitat look for the rare red-striped octopus. A variety of brilliantly colored nudibranchs are among literally hundreds that live in PNG waters. A count of nudibranchs at Madang revealed more than 500 species, about a third of which were undescribed.

Cuttlefish

111 Mad Dog Reef

Huge dogtooth tuna and sea turtles have been observed mating here. Schools of bigeye and silver jacks are common at the drop-off and clouds of black snappers roam in shoals along the lower wall. Immense soft corals and cotton candy corals cover the tip and attract everything from tiny dragonets to roaming bignose unicornfish. Look for dragonets in the rubble of the upper reef area. Fish appear here in clouds and then move on, creat-

Location: Northwestern Long Island

Depth Range: 6-40m (20-130ft) plus

Access: Boat

Expertise Rating: Advanced

ing a spectacular, ever-changing underwater show.

112 Bagabag Bay

This pleasant dive in a secluded and protected bay offers a look at some immense yellow elephant ear sponges. Many are covered in tiny, white sea cucumbers. Small gobies also move around these wavy sponges.

Location: Northwestern Bagabag

Depth Range: 3-8m (10-26ft) plus

Access: Boat

Expertise Rating: Novice

A goby rests on an elephant ear sponge.

Cuttlefish and pipefish live in the branching corals. Sea turtles are often seen sleeping along the slope.

At the reeftop look for schools of razorfish. Be aware of the occasional tidal currents in the deeper parts, where the sponges thrive.

113 Bagabag Wall

Hang on to your regulators! This drift dive is fun, fast and scenic. Eagle rays, turtles and large gorgonian sea fans are regularly seen along this steep, clear drop-off. Best dived in the afternoon when illuminated by the western sun, the wall can bring many surprises. Keep an eye on the deep blue for pelagic action.

Location: Western Bagabag

Depth Range: 6-40m (20-130ft) plus

Access: Boat

Expertise Rating: Advanced

114 Barracuda Seamount

Schools of barracuda, big tuna and swift rainbow runners are all part of the fare at this loaf-shaped reef that runs parallel to Bagabag in the open sea.

Location: Western Bagabag

Depth Range: 12-40m (40-130ft) plus

Access: Boat

Expertise Rating: Advanced

There seems to be an endless parade of Spanish mackerel when the current is running strong. The mackerel will come surprisingly close to stationary divers. This reef comes up from deep water but still near to shore and the pelagic life can be quite good when the tide is out-going.

The upper reef has some magnificent hard corals including big table corals and large antler corals. Swim to the tip and then drift back along the sloping wall.

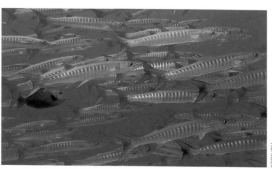

Barracuda show up when the current is running or at tide change.

115 Western Drop-Off

Pocked by fingers and cuts along the quickly sloping wall, this site can produce a current-swept ride that can challenge even the most experienced divers. Sea whips bending in the currents and dogtooth tuna struggling to hold place are just some of the sights that will greet you when you jump in here at tide change.

Location: Western Bagabag

Depth Range: 6-40m (20-130ft) plus

Access: Boat

Expertise Rating: Advanced

The canyons are a refuge from the sweep of the current. Here smaller creatures like colorful nudibranchs and anemonefish take shelter.

End the dive by turning into a small bay or carry on down the wall. The bay has some interesting corals and very clear water. Look for turtles near the mouth. Dolphins frequent the southern side of the bay and outer wall and can be heard sounding underwater.

A leopard chromodoris nudibranch.

TIM ROCK

Marine Life

The marine life in PNG is renowned for its biodiversity; this is one of the richest marine realms in the world. Although it would be impossible to record all the species you are likely to see while diving in PNG, this section will identify some of the more common marine life, along with some of interesting creatures that are difficult to find elsewhere in the world. Following that you'll find photos and descriptions of the potentially harmful or dangerous marine life you might encounter while diving in PNG.

One note on classification and nomenclature: common names are used freely by most divers but are notoriously inaccurate and inconsistent. The scientific name is more precise and consists of the *genus*—the name for a group of species that share a common ancestor—and the *species*, which includes only animals that are capable of breeding with each other.

For example, cabbage coral is also commonly called lettuce coral and chalice coral. Cabbage coral has the scientific name *Turbinaria reniformis*. The Latin word *reniform* means kidney-shaped—the scientist who described it thought the coral plates looked like kidneys not cabbage leaves.

Common Fish

Bennett's butterflyfish
Chaetodon bennetti

blue-girdled angelfish
Pomacanthus navarchus

bluefin trevally
Caranx melampygus

bluelined sea bream
Symphorichthys spilurus

clown triggerfish
Balistoides conspicillum

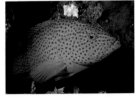

coral hind
Cephalopholis miniata

PHOTOS BY BOB HALSTEAD

152

dogtooth tuna
Gymnosarda unicolor

Emperor angelfish (juvenile)
Pomacanthus imperator

filiment-fin parrotfish
Scarus altipinnis

harlequin sweetlips
Plectorhinchus chaetodonoides

longfin bannerfish
Heniochus acuminatus

longnose hawkfish
Oxycirrhites typus

purple-headed sand tilefish
Hoplolatilus starcki

Randall's prawn-goby
Amblyeleotris randalli

red-banded wrasse
Cheilinus fasciatus

royal dottyback
Pseudochromis paccagnellae

saddleback anemonefish
Amphiprion polymnus

Seale's cardinalfish
Apogon sealei

squarespot anthias (male)
Pseudanthias pleurotaenia

white-margin unicornfish
Naso annulatus

yellowfin goatfish
Mulloidichthys vanicolensis

Common Invertebrates

barrel sponge
Xestospongia testudinaria

broadclub cuttlefish
Sepia latimanus

cabbage coral
Turbinaria reniformis

chambered nautilus
Nautilus pompilius

coral shrimp
Rhychocinetes sp.

egg cowrie
Aclyvolva sp.

eye cowrie
Cypraea argus

feather stars
Comanthina schlegeli

flatworm
Pseudoceros sp.

knob coral
Pocillipora sp.

lace coral
Stylaster sp.

mantis shrimp
Odontodactylus scyallarus

olive sea whips
Junceella sp.

plate coral
Acropora sp.

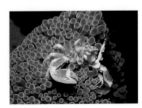

porcelain crab
Neopetrolisthes sp.

sea cucumber
Bohadschia argus

sea fan
Muricella sp.

sea star
Echinaster callosus

spiny lobster
Panulirus versicolor

staghorn coral
Acropora sp.

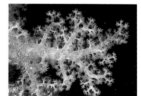

tree coral
Dendronephthya sp.

Unusual Fish & Invertebrates

comet fish
Calloplesiops altivelis

flamboyant cuttlefish
Metasepia pfefferi

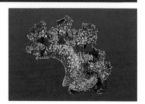

giant melibe
Melibe fimbriata

hump-headed spadefish (juvenile)
Platax batavianus

polychaete worm
Eunice sp.

scarlet cleaner shrimp
Lysmata debelius

short dragonfish
Eurypegasus draconis

striped frogfish
Antennarius striatus

tiger-striped garden eel
Heteroconger polyzona

Hazardous Marine Life

Marine creatures almost never attack divers, but many are well able to defend themselves if divers molest them either deliberately or inadvertently. Only in this circumstance, are divers likely to be injured. The ability to recognize hazardous creatures and stay clear is a valuable asset in avoiding accident and injury. The following are some of the most hazardous creatures found in PNG.

Stinging (fire) Corals

Fire corals come in a variety of shapes and can deliver a venomous sting when the nematocysts discharge, causing a burning sensation, or welts, on the skin. Avoid touching all corals. If you inadvertently brush against fire coral, do not try to rub the area as you will spread the stinging particles. Treat stings with vinegar, and antihistamine cream will help kill the pain.

Corallimorpharians

Corallimorpharians deliver a powerful sting by means of their large nematocysts. Learn to recognize corallimorpharians and do not touch. The initial sting, which may penetrate a Lycra suit, is not particularly painful but secondary symptoms, including neuritis (pain and impaired sensory perception) may occur. If stung you should seek medical aid.

Jellyfish

Jellyfish stings are released by nematocysts contained in their trailing tentacles. As a

rule, the longer the tentacles, the more painful the sting. Look out for jellyfish with trailing tentacles, particularly near the surface and at night, close to the boat. Stings are often irritating and not painful, but should be treated immediately with vinegar. Gently remove remaining tentacles. Beware that some people may have a stronger reaction than others, in which case you should prepare to resuscitate and seek medical aid.

PHOTOS BY BOB HALSTEAD

Cone Shells

Cone shells can deliver a venomous sting by shooting a tiny poison dart from their funnel-like proboscis. Do not touch cone shells. Stings will cause numbness and can be followed by muscle paralysis, or even respiratory paralysis and heart failure. If someone is stung, immobilize, apply a pressure bandage, be prepared to perform CPR and seek urgent medical aid.

Blue-Ringed Octopus

The blue-ringed octopus can deliver a venomous bite, which can result in paralysis. If a bite occurs, wash the wound, immobilize the victim, apply a pressure bandage and be prepared to perform CPR. Seek urgent medical aid.

Sea Urchins

Some sea urchins have sharp spines covered in venom. As with most hazardous critters, you can completely avoid injury if you don't touch. If an injury occurs, be prepared to administer CPR until the pain subsides. Antibiotics may be required, together with surgical removal of the spines.

Crown-of-Thorns

The crown-of-thorns sea star has venomous spines and can deliver a painful sting even if it's been dead for two or three days. To treat stings, remove any loose spines, soak stung area in hot water for 60-90 minutes and seek medical aid. Neglected wounds may produce serious injury. Even if you've been stung before, your reaction to another sting may be worse than the first.

Lionfish

Lionfish inject venom through hollow dorsal spines that can penetrate booties, wetsuits and leather gloves. Lionfish wounds can cause intense pain but can be avoided if you are careful not to step on or touch them. To treat, wash the wound, immerse in hot water for 60-90 minutes, seek medical aid.

Scorpionfish

Scorpionfish and stonefish also inject venom through hollow dorsal spines. Again, injury can be completely avoided if you avoid contact, but beware, these fish can look remarkably similar to rockfish. To treat an injury, wash the wound and immerse in hot water for 30-90 minutes, and seek medical aid.

Sea Snakes

Sea snakes rarely bite even if they are handled, but avoid touching them as they are capable of injecting powerful venom. To treat a sea snake bite, use a pressure bandage and immobilize the victim. Try to identify the snake, be prepared to administer CPR and send for urgent medical aid.

Sharks

Tropical shark attacks are invariably mistakes. Avoid spearfishing, carrying fish baits or mimicking a wounded fish and the likelihood of being attacked will greatly diminish. Face and quietly watch any shark that is acting aggressively and be prepared to push it away with camera, knife or tank. If someone is bitten by a shark, stop the bleeding, reassure the patient, treat for shock, send for immediate medical aid.

Crocodiles

Crocodile encounters with divers are extremely rare but take caution exploring new areas close to mangroves or river mouths. If in doubt ask local villagers if crocodiles are present. Do not dive if large crocodiles are in the area. If a bite occurs, stop any bleeding, reassure the patient, treat for shock, send for immediate medical aid.

Basic First Aid Procedures

The measures described below are basic first aid using commonly available materials and equipment, and are not a substitute for medical attention. The seriousness of an encounter with a hazardous marine animal depends not only on the nature of the animal but on the location of the wound—a bite, spine or sting near the eyes is a very different thing than one to a calloused heel.

1. Immediately, in the water if possible, insure that the victim is breathing. If not, make sure the airway is clear and begin mouth-to-mouth resuscitation. Remove the victim from the water as quickly as possible, check for breathing and heartbeat, begin CPR if necessary.

2. To minimize shock, place the victim in a head-down position; minimize blood loss by applying pressure and/or a tourniquet and elevate the limb involved.

3. Try to remove spiracles, spines, or bristles with tweezers or adhesive tape, but leave any that are deeply embedded (in joints, near eyes, or near major blood vessels) for surgical removal later. Wash the area with sterile (boiled) water. If a sponge is thought to be involved, soak the area with vinegar diluted with an equal volume of sterile water. Venom and pain may be reduced by heating the afflicted area with warm water or a hot hair drier.

4. If a creature with nematocysts was involved, the sting should be washed out with sea water. (Do not use fresh water, as nematocysts will trigger in defense of something "unnatural" to them; fresh water may in fact result in additional stings.) Flood the area with diluted vinegar and remove any visible nematocysts with a pair of tweezers. Apply shaving cream to the site, and carefully scrape it with a razor or knife. Flood the area again with diluted vinegar, followed by several teaspoons of baking soda (sodium bicarbonate) dissolved in sterile water. Make sure nematocysts are not spread to other areas—especially the eyes—or other people.

5. Apply a topical antibiotic such as bacitracin or neomycin if available. Place a sterile dressing over the wound—a section cut from a clean cotton T-shirt or wash-cloth, boiled and then dried will do fine—and secure it with tape or string.

Diving Conservation & Awareness

BOB HALSTEAD

PNG Divers' Association

Currently no official marine reserves exist in PNG, but there continues to be a number of movements and some legislation moving toward this goal. PNG is blessed with concerned dive operators who appreciate and strive for long-term protection of the resources on which their businesses thrive.

To promote rational, responsible growth of the dive tourism industry and to ensure the conservation of PNG's diving resources, dive tour operators formed the **Papua New Guinea Diver's Association** (PNGDA). Members of the PNGDA agreed on the following code of ethics:

"At a time when coral reefs worldwide are under threat, the PNGDA recognizes the exceptional quality of PNG's natural marine resources and their importance for both village life and the Nation, and pledges that the Association will do everything in its power to ensure that these resources, including the sea bed, reefs, wrecks and the marine life that lives on them and in the waters surrounding them, will be conserved."

Contact PNGDA

P.O. Box 1646
Port Moresby, PNG
☎ 320 0211
Fax: 320 0223
tourismpng@dg.com.pg

Responsible Diving

Dive sites tend to be located where the reefs and walls display the most beautiful corals and sponges. It only takes a moment—an inadvertently placed hand or knee on the coral or an unaware brush or kick with a fin—to destroy this fragile, living part of our delicate ecosystem. Please consider the following tips when diving and help preserve the ecology and beauty of the reefs:

1. Maintain proper buoyancy control and avoid over-weighting. Be aware that buoyancy can change over the period of an extended trip: initially you may breathe harder and need more weighting; a few days later you may breath more easily and need less weight.

2. Use correct weight belt position to stay horizontal, i.e., raise the belt above your waist to elevate your feet/fins, and move it lower toward your hips to lower them.

3. Use your tank position as a balance weight, i.e., raise your backpack on the tank to lower your legs, and lower the backpack on the tank to raise your legs.

4. Be careful about buoyancy loss at depth; the deeper you go the more your wetsuit compresses, and the more buoyancy you lose.

5. Photographers must be extra careful. Cameras and equipment affect buoyancy. Changing f-stops, framing a subject, and maintaining position for a photo often conspire to prohibit the ideal "no-touch" approach on a reef. So, when you must use "holdfasts," choose them intelligently (i.e., use one finger only for leverage off an area of dead coral).

6. Avoid full leg kicks when working close to the bottom and when leaving a photo scene. When you inadvertently kick something, stop kicking! Seems obvious, but some divers either semi-panic or are totally oblivious when they bump something. When treading water in shallow reef areas, take care not to kick up clouds of sand. Settling sand can easily smother the delicate organisms of the reef.

7. When swimming in strong currents, be extra careful about leg kicks and handholds.

8. Attach dangling gauges, computer consoles, and octopus regulators. They are like miniature wrecking balls to a reef.

9. Never drop boat anchors onto a coral reef, and take care not to ground boats on coral. Encourage dive operators and regulatory bodies to establish permanent moorings at popular dive sites.

10. Resist the temptation to collect or buy corals or shells. Aside from the ecological damage, taking home marine souvenirs depletes the beauty of a site and spoils the enjoyment of others.

11. Resist the temptation to feed fish. You may disturb their normal eating habits, encourage aggressive behavior, or feed them food that is detrimental to their health.

Marine Conservation Organizations

Coral reefs and oceans are facing unprecedented environmental pressures. The following groups are actively involved in promoting responsible diving practices, publicizing environmental marine threats, and lobbying for better policies.

CORAL: The Coral Reef Alliance
☎ 510-848-0110
www.coral.org/

Coral Forest
☎ 415-788-REEF
www.blacktop.com/coralforest/

Cousteau Society
☎ 757-523-9335
www.cousteau.org

Project AWARE Foundatio
☎ 714-540-0251
www.projectaware.org

ReefKeeper International
☎ 305-358-4600
www.reefkeeper.org

Look, admire but leave behind.

Listings

Telephone Calls

To call PNG, dial the international access code for the country you are calling from (in the U.S. it's 011), + 675 (PNG's country code) + the 7-digit local number.

Accommodations

Port Moresby Area

Airways Hotel
(181 rooms)
P.O. Box 1942, Boroko, PNG
☎ 324 5200 Fax: 325 0759
Air-conditioned rooms, telephone, swimming pool, bars, 2 restaurants (1 fine dining with live jazz piano), sports and recreation area, gift shop, tours arranged, car rental, airport transfers

Amber's Inn
(22 rooms)
P.O. Box 1139, Boroko, PNG
☎ 325 0624 Fax: 325 9565
Some rooms air-conditioned and en suite, some with fan and shared facilities, swimming pool, bar, restaurant, car rental, airport transfers

Ela Beach Hotel
(47 rooms)
P.O. Box 813, Port Moresby
☎ 321 2100 Fax: 321 2434
On beach, air-conditioned rooms, TV, telephone, swimming pool, bar restaurant, airport transfers, dive shop and instructor on premises

Gateway Hotel
(96 rooms)
P.O. Box 1215, Boroko, PNG
☎ 325 3855 Fax: 325 4585
Air-conditioned rooms, TV, telephone, mini bar, 4 bars, 2 restaurants, conference facilities, car rental, airport transfers

Granville Motel
(134 rooms, 10 units)
P.O. Box 1246, Boroko, PNG
☎ 325 7155 Fax: 325 7672
Air-conditioned rooms, TV, swimming pool, bar, restaurant, car rental, conference facilities, airport transfers

Islander Travelodge
(165 rooms)
P.O. Box 1981, Boroko, PNG
☎ 325 5955/3196 Fax: 325 0837
Air-conditioned rooms, TV, telephone, 2 bars, restaurant, swimming pool, conference facilities, sports complex, airport transfers

Loloata Island Resort
(17 rooms)
P.O. Box 5290, Boroko, PNG
☎ 325 8590/1369 Fax: 325 8933
loloata@daltron.com.pg
www.loloata.com
Private island. Cost includes all meals. Air-conditioned rooms, bar, gift shop, windsurfing, kayaking, swimming, fishing. Conference facilities, courtesy bus to Port Moresby and airport, dive shop, instruction and dive boat

Port Moresby Travelodge
(175 rooms, 2 suites)
P.O. Box 1661, Port Moresby, PNG
☎ 321 2266/1987 Fax: 321 7534
Air-conditioned rooms, TV, telephone, swimming pool, sports facilities, bar, 2 restaurants, gift shop, car rental, airport transfers

Milne Bay

Masurina Lodge
(40 rooms)
P.O. Box 5, Alotau, PNG
☎ 641 1212 Fax: 641 1406/1286
A guesthouse with meals included in the tariff, 30 air-conditioned rooms with en suite, 10 with fans and shared facilities, bar and dining room, conference facilities, car rental, airport transfers

Veawai Melanesian Resort
(18 rooms)
P.O. Box 240, Alotau, PNG
☎ 641 0255 Fax: 641 0266
Air-conditioned rooms, TV, mini fridge, telephone, bar, restaurant, swimming pool, airport transfers

D'Entrecasteau Islands & Tufi

Tufi Dive Resort
(7 double rooms)
P.O. Box 684, Port Moresby, PNG
☎ 321 7647 Fax: 321 7640 www.tufi.com

Bar, restaurant, local tours, dive facility, instruction, 2 dive boats, airport transfers, deck with spectacular fjord views

Lae

Lae International Hotel
(97 rooms, 3 suites)
P.O. Box 2774, Lae, PNG
☎ 472 2000 Fax: 472 2534
Air-conditioned rooms, TV, telephone, 2 bars, 2 restaurants, conference facilities, swimming pool, sports facilities, gift shop, car rental, tours arranged, airport transfers

Huon Gulf Lodge
(30 rooms)
P.O. Box 612, Lae, PNG

☎ 472 4844 Fax: 472 5023
Air-conditioned rooms, TV, bar, fridge, telephone, swimming pool, 2 bars, dining room

Melanesian Hotel
(65 rooms)
P.O. Box 756, Lae, PNG
☎ 472 3744 Fax: 472 3706
Air-conditioned rooms, TV, telephone, mini bar, bar, 2 restaurants, 2 swimming pools, conference facilities, access to botanical gardens

Madang

Coastwatcher Hotel
(40 rooms)
P.O. Box 324, Madang, PNG
☎ 852 2684 Fax: 852 2716
Air-conditioned rooms, TV, telephone, fridge, swimming pool, bar and restaurant, private party facilities, 2 conference rooms, car rental, tours, dive trips arranged, airport transfers

Jais Aben Resort
(18 units)
P.O. Box 105, Madang, PNG
☎ 852 3311 Fax: 852 3560
On Nagada Harbour, island views, self-catering rooms have private facilities and air-conditioning, bar, restaurant, conference facilities, dive shop, instruction and boats, general water sports, tour bus, airport transfers

Madang Resort Hotel
(68 rooms and suites)
P.O. Box 707, Madang, PNG

☎ 852 2766 Fax: 852 3543
Air-conditioned rooms from budget to suites, TV, telephone, bar, 2 restaurants, water views, conference facilities, swimming pool, dive shop, instruction, dive boats, car rental, artifact gallery, gardens, airport transfers; base for Melanesian Tourist Services and MV *Melanesian Discoverer*

Malolo Plantation Lodge
(14 rooms)
P.O. Box 413, Madang, PNG
☎ 852 1662
or c/o
Trans Niugini Tours
P.O. Box 371, Mt. Hagen, PNG
☎ 542 1438 Fax: 542 2470
42km from Madang along north coast road, on beach, air-conditioned rooms, swimming pool, gardens, bar, restaurant, conference facilities, dive shop, instruction, nitrox

Smuggler's Inn
(38 rooms, 2 suites)
P.O. Box 303, Madang, PNG
☎ 852 2267 Fax: 852 2744

On beach, air-conditioned rooms, TV, telephone, swimming pool, bar, restaurant, gift shop, conference facilities, car rental, dive shop, instruction, tours, watersports, airport transfers

Kimbe Bay

Palm Lodge Hoskins
(24 rooms)
P.O. Box 10, Hoskins, PNG
☎ 983 5113 Fax: 983 5015
On beach, air-conditioned rooms, swimming pool, bar, restaurant, car rental

Walindi Plantation Resort
(12 rooms)
P.O. Box 4
Kimbe, W.N.B.P., PNG
☎ 983 5441/5466 Fax 983 5638
Beach bungalows and plantation house, pool, tennis court, restaurant, bar, dive operation, photographic services

Rabaul

Hamamas Hotel
(32 rooms)
P.O. Box 214, Rabaul, PNG
☎ 982 1999 Fax: 982 1970
Air-conditioned rooms, TV, fridge, function room, restaurant and bars, swimming pool, gardens, tours and dive trips arranged, VIP guest lounge at airport and shuttle bus around town

Kaivuna Resort Hotel
(30 rooms)
P.O. Box 395, Rabaul, PNG
☎ 982 1766 Fax: 982 1767

Air-conditioned rooms, TV, swimming pool, bar, restaurant, conference facilities, dive trips arranged, volcano views, tours

Kulau Beach Resort
(10 beach cottage rooms and 7 deluxe apartments)
P.O. Box 65, Rabaul, PNG
☎ 982 7222 Fax: 982 7226
On the shores of Talili Bay near Rabaul town, air-conditioned rooms, TV, telephone, bar, restaurant, watersports, dive shop, instruction, dive boats and trips

Kavieng

Kavieng Hotel
(20 en suite rooms, 14 budget rooms)
P.O. Box 4, Kavieng, PNG
☎ 984 2199 Fax: 984 2283
Air-conditioned rooms with en suite, budget rooms with fan and shared facilities, telephone, TV, swimming pool, bar, restaurant, car rental, airport transfers

Lissenung Island Resort
(2 bungalows with 2 rooms each)
P.O. Box 536 Kavieng, PNG
☎/Fax: 984 2526
Small private island 15-minute boat ride from Kavieng town. Comfortable basic accommodations, shore diving, boats, instruction, diving tours to the main dive sites in the Kavieng area

Malign Lodge
(16 rooms)
P.O. Box 238, Kavieng, PNG
☎ 984 2344 Fax: 984 2452
On beach, air-conditioned deluxe rooms, telephone, TV, bar restaurant, conference facilities, gift shop, dive shop, boats, instruction, dive tours, airport transfers

Mansava Adventure Lodge (Tsoi Island)
(5 rooms)
P.O. Box 419, Kavieng, PNG
☎ 984 1441 Fax: 984 2254
Village-style resort (no electricity), rooms with double and single beds, kerosene lamps, cooking facilities, transport provided, village, canoeing, fishing and diving tours arranged

Diving Services

Archipelago Diving
P.O. Box 479, Kavieng, PNG
☎ 984 2531 Fax: 984 2531
archipelago@global.net.pg
www.archipelagodiving.com.au
Sales & Rentals: Full equipment and camera rental and sales
Credit Cards: Most major credit cards
Boats: 3 dive boats from 7 to 12m
Passengers: maximum 12 divers
Courses: PADI courses from Open Water to Assistant Instructor
Trips: 2- and 3-tank trips to popular and unusual sites
Other: Small land-based operation catering to individuals or groups of up to 10 divers staying at the local hotels; can organize hotel/dive packages and overnight stays on nearby islands or in villages close to the dive sites; boat, fishing charters and land tours

Dive Centre - Solatai
Ela Beach Hotel
P.O. Box 813, Port Moresby
☎ 321 2100 Fax: 321 2434
Sales & Rentals: Small dive shop stocks and services top-name equipment, rental gear available
Credit Cards: Most major credit cards
Boats: 1 fast sun-shaded outboard-powered dive boat for 8 divers out of Port Moresby; 1 diesel-powered dive boat with a large compressor for 20 divers out of Bootless Inlet
Trips: Bootless Bay and Sunken Barrier excursions
Courses: PADI dive courses from Open Water to Divemaster by prior arrangement

Jais Aben Resort
P.O. Box 105, Madang, PNG
☎ 852 3311 Fax: 852 3560
jaisaben@global.net.pg
Sales & Rentals: Full rentals; sales include masks, fins, snorkels, spare parts, including lenses
Credit Cards: Most major credit cards
Boats: 2 7m high-speed dive boats (8 divers each)
Trips: Local trips and offshore islands
Courses: PADI Open Water to Divemaster
Other: Some equipment servicing available; 3-tank day trips and night dives, to reefs, walls, drop-offs and wrecks

Kulau Beach Resort
P.O. Box 65, Rabaul, PNG
☎ 982 7222 Fax: 982 7226
Sales & Rentals: Sales and full rentals available from Dive Rabaul dive shop
Credit Cards: Most major credit cards
Boats: 3 10-passenger boats, 1 6-passenger boat
Trips: Rabaul, Simpson Harbor, Gazelle Peninsula, Watom Island
Courses: PADI courses
Other: Long established resort and dive operation. Owner is a very experienced diver and over the years has collected and sunk some derelict vessels in front of the resort; two on-site compressors

Lissenung Diving
P.O. Box 536 Kavieng, PNG
☎/Fax: 984 2526
Lissenung@global.net.pg; Petamo@aol.com
www.diversionOZ.com
Sales & Rentals: 10 full sets scuba equipment for rent; no sales
Credit Cards: Not accepted; travelers checks OK
Boats: 1 27ft (6 divers), 1 23ft (6 divers)
Trips: To all popular sites, 1-3-tank dives; night dives in front of Lissenung Island Resort
Courses: All PADI courses, plus additional 10 specialty courses
Other: Shore diving for divers staying at Lissenung Island Resort. Free pickup and gear storage for divers staying in Kavieng

Loloata Island Resort
P.O. Box 5290, Boroko, PNG
☎ 325 8590 Fax: 852 8933
loloata@daltron.com.pg
www.loloata.com
Sales & Rentals: Limited sales. Full rental equipment; service & repairs to most major brands
Credit Cards: Most major credit cards
Boats: 1 9m aluminum dive boat with freshwater shower, camera wash, for 9 divers max; 1 7m fully covered fiberglass banana boat for 6 divers
Trips: 2-tank morning dives and 1-tank afternoon dive. Night dives on request for 2 or more divers
Courses: PADI Discover Scuba to Divemaster certification by prior arrangement

Other: Range of approx. 30 dive sites on outer reef walls, pinnacles and channels, inner reef patches, wrecks and muck. An intimate resort 20 minutes from the international airport providing comfortable over-the-water accommodation in Bootless Bay. Excellent alternative to staying in Port Moresby

Malagan Diving

P.O.Box 238, Kavieng, PNG
☎ 852 2766 Fax: 852 3543
melanesian@meltours.com
www.meltours.com
Sales & Rentals: Full scuba equipment line for rent; limited sales
Credit Cards: Most major credit cards
Boats: 1 boat sized to carry 6 divers
Trips: 2-3 daily to popular dive sites, including coral reefs, drop-offs, walls, sharks and large pelagics and night dives
Courses: None
Other: Located on the grounds of Malign Lodge

Malolo Plantation Lodge

P.O. Box 371, Mt. Hagen, PNG
☎ 542 1438 Fax: 542 2470
800-521-7242 (U.S.)
travel@pngtours.com
www.pngtours.com
Sales & Rentals: Rentals available from the dive shop
Credit Cards: Most major credit cards
Boats: 1 aluminum boat with canopy, sized to carry 16 divers
Trips: North Madang coast and Bagabag and KarKar Islands. Also WWII shipwrecks & planes, channels, seamounts and pelagic dives. Land-based dives and specialty dives available, nitrox
Courses: PADI, T.D.I & I.A.N.T.D., nitrox

Niugini Diving Adventures

Coastwatchers Dr.
P.O. Box 707, Madang, PNG
☎ 852 2766 Fax: 852 3543
melanesian@meltours.com
www.meltours.com
Sales & Rentals: full scuba equipment for rent; limited sales

Credit Cards: Most major credit cards
Boats: 2 boats sized to carry 20 divers each
Trips: 2-3 daily to popular dive sites including coral reefs, drop-offs, walls, wrecks, sharks and large pelagics and night dives
Courses: All PADI courses
Other: Located on the grounds of Madang Resort Hotel

Tufi Dive Resort

P.O. Box 684, Port Moresby, PNG
☎ 321 7647 Fax: 321 7640
www.tufi.com
Sales & Rentals: Rentals available
Credit Cards: Most major credit cards
Boats: 2 sun-shaded, outboard-powered banana boats, each sized to carry 6 divers, 1 large, diesel-powered boat for 12 divers or overnight for small groups
Trips: Outer reefs and drop-offs, fjord diving and snorkeling, WWII wrecks
Courses: Resort, Open Water and others by prior arrangement
Other: Owned and operated by PADI Instructor Ken Weaving. Tufi Dive Resort can arrange for visitors to spend a night in a village guesthouse and enjoy a traditional meal. The resort is equipped to handle up to 12 divers

Walindi Photo

P.O. Box 4, Kimbe, W.N.B.P., PNG
☎ 983 4386 Fax: 983 4386/5638
tammy@walindi.com
www.walindi.com
Sales & Rentals: Ikelite dealer; rentals include Nikonos V cameras & lenses, housed Nikon N90s, Ikelite and Nikonos strobes, housed Hi-8 & digital video cameras (PAL and NTSC), dive computers
Credit Cards: Most major credit cards
Boats: (see Walindi Resort); also photo courses on live-aboards *FeBrina* and *Star Dancer*
Trips: Kimbe Bay and specialized photo trips to suite the photographer
Courses: PADI certification, underwater photography & video courses, advanced photography workshops
Other: Photo pro is well-known photojournalist Tammy Peluso. E6 slide processing, video editing and custom video and photo shoots available

Walindi Resort

P.O. Box 4, Kimbe, W.N.B.P., PNG
☎ 983 5441/5466 Fax: 983 5638
walindi@datec.com.pg
www.walindi.com
Sales & Rentals: Full range of scuba and snorkeling gear for rent, camera rentals through Walindi Photo; limited sales
Credit Cards: Most major credit cards

Boats: 1 7m (4 passengers), 1 7m (6 passengers), 1 10m (10 passengers)
Trips: 2- or 3-tank dives, night dives to moored sites
Courses: PADI courses by prior arrangement
Other: Walindi is considered to be a "must dive" destination for serious underwater photographers and specializes in sea mammal action

Live-Aboards

Barbarian II

P.O. Box 320, Lae, PNG
☎ 472 5692 Fax: 472 2455
Vessel ☎ 872 761 339 154 Vessel Fax: 872 761 339 155
niuginidive@global.net.pg
Home port: Lae
Description: Displacement hull, 14m
Accommodations: 6 person, twin-share
Destinations: Southeast coast of PNG mainland to Lae, Tami Islands, Tufi and Milne Bay
Duration: 7-10 days
Season: year round
Passengers: 6
Other: Owner Rodney Pearce is one of the pioneers of PNG sport diving and has discovered many WWII wrecks. Appeals to experienced divers on a limited budget. Custom charters available.

MV Chertan

Milne Bay Charters
P.O. Box 176, Alotau M.B.P., PNG
☎ 641 1167 Fax: 641 1291
Vessel ☎ 145 114 619

Mvchertain@bigpond.com
www.chertan.com
Home port: Alotau
Description: 18m fiberglass
Accommodations: 6 air-conditioned twinshare cabins
Destinations: All reefs in Milne Bay, including Nuakata, Furgusson and Normanby Islands, and the North Coast.
Duration: 5-14 days
Season: Milne Bay year round
Passengers: 12

MV FeBrina

P.O. Box 4, Kimbe, W.N.B.P., PNG
☎ 983 5441/5466 Fax: 983 5638
info@Febrina.com
www.febrina.com
Home port: Walindi
Description: 22m steel
Accommodations: 7 double cabins, 6 twinshare cabins
Destinations: Kimbe Bay, Kavieng; also the Father Reefs near Lolobau Island, the Bali-Vitu group of islands north of the Willaumez Peninsula, and south coast of West New Britain
Duration: 5-12 days
Season: Kimbe Bay and Kavieng year round
Passengers: 13
Other: E6 processing available

MV *Golden Dawn*

Dolphin Enterprises
P.O. Box 1335, Port Moresby, PNG
☎ 325 6500 Fax: 325 0302
Vessel ☎ 61 1 45119159 Fax: 61 1 45219159
dive@MVGoldenDawn.com
www.MVGoldenDawn.com
Home port: Port Moresby
Description: 24m single hull, steel
Equipment: Air conditioned, watermaker, static and dynamic stabilizers, 2 inflatable tenders; satellite phone, fax and email available
Accommodations: 5 en suite cabins
Destinations: Eastern Fields, Wewak, Hermit & Ninigos, Crown and Long Islands, exploratory
Duration: Usually around 10 days
Season: Year round
Passengers: 10
Other: Offers land excursions, on-board water purifyer

MV *Moonlighting*

Blue Sea Charters
P.O. Box 1071, Madang, PNG
☎ 852 3302 Fax: 852 3540
ldempster@global.net.pg
www.blueseacharters.com
Home port: Madang
Description: Grand Banks 50
Accommodations: 6 person, 3 twin-share cabins
Destinations: Madang, Hansa Bay, Karkar, Long & Crown Islands
Duration: 4, 7 and 10 days
Season: Year round
Passengers: 6
Other: Fully air-conditioned, large sundeck, desalinator, saloon, airport transfer, 240V power points, land-based tours available

Melanesian Discoverer

Coastwatchers Dr.
P.O. Box 707, Madang, PNG
☎ 852 2766 Fax: 852 3543
melanesian@meltours.com
www.meltours.com
Home port: Madang
Description: 39m catamaran
Equipment: Air-conditioned, 3 decks, cocktail bar, observation lounge, inflatable tender
Accommodations: 22 en suite cabins
Destinations: Madang to Milne Bay
Duration: 7 days (diving & cultural land tours)
Season: Variable, Milne Bay, Wewak, Sepik River, Madang year round
Passengers: 42
Other: Not strictly a dive boat, but has daily trips to popular dive sites. Good for both divers and non-divers

Paradise Sport

Mike Ball Dive Expeditions
252 Walker St., Townsville QLD 4810
Australia
☎ 61 7 47723022 Fax: 61 7 47212152
800-852-4319 or 888-MIKE BALL (U.S. only)
mbde@mikeball.com
www.mikeball.com
Home port: Milne Bay/Kavieng
Description: 32m luxury catamaran
Accommodations: 2 king-sized suites with en suite, 6 standard suites with en suite, 2 economy doubles
Destinations: Milne Bay & Kavieng
Duration: 8-11-day trips
Season: Oct-May, Milne Bay; June-Sept, Kavieng
Passengers: 22
Other: E6 processing, video lab, photo pro on board, reef ecology certificate course

Star Dancer

Peter Hughes Diving, Inc.
1390 South Dixie Hwy. Suite 1109,
Coral Gables, FL 33146 U.S.
☎ 305 669 9391 Fax: 305 669 9475
800-932-6237 (U.S.)
dancer@peterhughes.com
www.peterhughes.com
Home port: Walindi & Rabaul
Description: 37m, 7m beam, aluminium tender
Accommodations: 2 master staterooms, 2 delux twin-share rooms, 1 owner suite; private heads in each room
Destinations: Kimbe Bay, Rabaul, Duke of York Islands, Witu Islands
Duration: 8- and 10-day trips
Season: April-Dec, Rabaul; Jan-March, Walindi
Passengers: 16
Other: E6 processing, photo pro on board, Open Water referrals and specialty courses

Tiata

P.O. Box 1745 Port Moresby, PNG
Fax: 325 9746
tiata@global.net.pg
www.diversion.com
Home port: Bootless Bay
Description: 20m timber construction
Equipment: Dynamic and static stabilizers, large capacity water-maker, inflatable tender
Accommodations: 5 cabins
Destinations: Kavieng, Milne Bay, East New Britain, New Hanover, exploratory
Season: Year round
Passengers: 10
Other: 240V & 120V charging tables, PADI courses

Clubs

The **Port Moresby Sub Aqua Club** also arranges day trips for its members and their guests using its own fast boat

P.O. Box 1488 Port Moresby, PNG
☎ 320 1200 Fax: 320 1257

Tourist Offices

Contact the following agencies to find out more about diving or topside activities in PNG:

Diversion Dive Travel
P.O. Box 7026, Cairns 4870,
Australia
☎ 61 7 40390200
Fax: 61 7 40390300
info@diversionOZ.com
www.diversionOZ.com

Melanesian Tourist Services
P.O. Box 707, Madang, PNG
☎ 852 2766 Fax: 852 3543
mts@meltours.com
www.meltours.com

Owen Coney's South Pacific Travel
☎ 323 5245 Fax: 323 5246
P.O. Box 195, Boroko, PNG

PNG Tourism Promotion Authority
P.O. Box 1291, Port Moresby, PNG
☎ 320 0211 Fax: 320 0223

Sea New Guinea
P.O. Box 7002, Sydney,
Australia 2001
☎ 61 2 92675563
Fax: 61 2 93676118
sng@dot.net.au

Trans Niugini Tours
P.O. Box 371, Mt. Hagen, PNG
☎ 542 1438 Fax: 542 2470
travel@pngtours.com
www.pngtours.com

Index

dive sites covered in this book appear in **bold** type

Lonely Planet Series Descriptions

Lonely Planet **travel guides** explore a destination in depth with options to suit a range of budgets. With reliable, practical advice on getting around, restaurants and accommodations, these easy-to-use guides also include detailed maps, color photographs, extensive background material and coverage of sites both on and off the beaten track.

For budget travelers **shoestring guides** are the best single source of travel information covering an entire continent or large region. Written by experienced travelers these 'tried and true' classics offer reliable, first-hand advice on transportation, restaurants and accommodations, and insider tips for avoiding bureaucratic confusion and stretching money as far as possible.

City guides cover many of the world's great cities with full-color photographs throughout, front and back cover gatefold maps, and information for every traveler's budget and style. With information for business travelers, all the best places to eat and shop and itinerary suggestions for long and short-term visitors, city guides are a complete package.

Lonely Planet **phrasebooks** have essential words and phrases to help travelers communicate with the locals. With color tabs for quick reference, an extensive vocabulary, use of local scripts and easy-to-follow pronunciation instructions, these handy, pocket-sized language guides cover most situations a traveler is likely to encounter.

Lonely Planet **walking guides** cover some of the world's most exciting trails. With detailed route descriptions including degrees of difficulty and best times to go, reliable maps and extensive background information, these guides are an invaluable resource for both independent hikers and those in organized groups.

Lonely Planet **travel atlases** are thoroughly researched and fact-checked by the guidebook authors to ensure they complement the books. And the handy format means none of the holes, wrinkles, tears, or constant folding and refolding of flat maps. They include background information in five languages.

Journeys is a new series of travel literature that captures the spirit of a place, illuminates a culture, recounts an adventure and introduces a fascinating way of life. Written by a diverse group of writers, they are tales to read while on the road or at home in your favorite armchair.

Entertaining, independent and adventurous, Lonely Planet **videos** encourage the same approach to travel as the guidebooks. Currently broadcast throughout the world, this award-winning series features all original footage and music.

Lonely Planet Pisces Books

The **Diving & Snorkeling** books are dive guides to top destinations worldwide. Beautifully illustrated with full-color photos throughout, the series explores the best diving and snorkeling areas and prepares divers for what to expect when they get there. Each site is described in detail, with information on suggested ability levels, depth, visibility, and, of course, marine life. There's basic topside information as well for each destination. Don't miss the guides to:

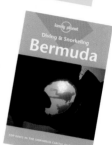

Australia: Coral Sea &
  Great Barrier Reef

Australia: Southeast Coast

Bahamas: Family Islands & Grand

Bahamas: Nassau &
  New Providence

Baja California

Bali & the Komodo Region

Belize

Bermuda

Best Caribbean Diving

Bonaire

British Virgin Islands

Cayman Islands

Cocos Island

Cozumel

Cuba

Curaçao

Fiji

Florida Keys

Guam & Yap

Hawaiian Islands

Jamaica

Northern California &
  Monterey Peninsula

Pacific Northwest

Palau

Papua New Guinea

Puerto Rico

Red Sea

Roatan & Honduras'
  Bay Islands

Scotland

Seychelles

Southern California

St. Maarten, Saba,
  & St. Eustatius

Texas

Truk Lagoon

Turks & Caicos

U.S. Virgin Islands

Vanuatu

Plus illustrated natural history guides:

Pisces Guide to Caribbean
  Reef Ecology

Great Reefs of the World

Sharks of Tropical &
  Temperate Seas

Venomous & Toxic
  Marine Life of
  the World

Watching Fishes

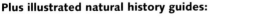

Where to Find Us . . .

Lonely Planet is known worldwide for publishing practical, reliable and no-nonsense travel information in our guides and on our web site. The Lonely Planet list covers just about every accessible part of the world. Currently there are nine series: *Pisces books, travel guides, shoestring guides, walking guides, city guides, phrasebooks, audio packs, travel atlases* and *Journeys*–a unique collection of travel writing.

Lonely Planet Publications

Australia
PO Box 617, Hawthorn 3122, Victoria
☎ (03) 9819 1877 fax (03) 9819 6459
e-mail talk2us@lonelyplanet.com.au

USA
150 Linden Street
Oakland, California 94607
☎ (510) 893 8555, (800) 275 8555
fax (510) 893 8563
e-mail info@lonelyplanet.com

UK
10A Spring Place,
London NW5 3BH
☎ (0171) 428 4800 fax (0171) 428 4828
e-mail go@lonelyplanet.co.uk

France
1 rue du Dahomey
75011 Paris
☎ 01 55 25 33 00 fax 01 55 25 33 01
e-mail bip@lonelyplanet.fr

World Wide Web: www.lonelyplanet.com or **AOL keyword: lp**